Weaving
a
Woman's Life

Weaving
a
Woman's Life

Spiritual Lessons from the Loom

Paula Chaffee Scardamalia

NETTLES & GREEN THREADS PRESS
Rensselaerville, New York

NETTLES & GREEN THREADS PRESS
P. O. Box 160
Rensselaerville, NY 12147

Scardamalia, Paula Chaffee.

Weaving a woman's life: spiritual lessons from the loom / Paula Chaffee Scardamalia. -- Rensselaerville, NY : Nettles & Green Threads Press, 2006.

p. ; cm.

ISBN-13: 978-0-9777775-0-1
ISBN-10: 0-9777775-0-2
Includes bibliographical references.

1. Women--Spiritual life. 2. Quality of life. 3. Spirituality. 4. Self-realization in women. 5. Weaving--Religious aspects. 6. Meditation. 7. Women--Psychology. I. Title.

BV4527. S23 2006   2006922088
248.8/43--dc22   0604

Printed in the United States of America
10 9 8 7 6 5 4 3 2 1

Cover photo by Stephen Vincent Scardamalia
www.svsphotography.com

Loom illustrations courtesy of Schact Spindle Company, Inc.
www.schactspindle.com

Cover and interior design by To The Point Solutions
www.tothepointsolutions.com

This book is dedicated to three of my Muses
who also happen to be sisters,
Indira, Sandy, and Pat, my mom,
who continues to inspire me from the other side,

And

To the man who always does everything in his power
To help me weave a life of beauty and love,
Best friend, lover, and husband,
Bob

$\mathcal{C}ontents$

Contents

Acknowledgements

THE JOURNEY OF THIS BOOK BEGAN AT THE MAUI Writer's Conference in 2002 when literary agent, Debra Goldstein, of Creative Cultures, Inc., sat across from me at a consultation table and asked me if I had ever considered doing a book on something like "Lessons from the Loom." It was one of those lightning bolt moments, and I will be forever grateful to Debra for acting as midwife through three years of first giving birth to the original proposal and then trying to find it a publishing home. When we couldn't find an established home for it, she told me to do it myself. So I have, and I thank her for her encouragement and support.

A special thank you to my niece, Leslie McIlroy, for writing the poem that begins this book. She is a fine poet and a mother of great heart and courage.

I am also grateful to my circle of writing friends who provided encouragement, support, feedback and editing, especially my sisters of the International Women Writers' Guild: Liz Aleshire, who first taught me how to prepare a book proposal, and then used her red pen with accuracy and insight to edit my finished manuscript; Marsha McGregor, who read and edited several chapters through the eyes of her wise and loving soul; Sheila Weinstein and Jennifer Ortiz, who were present for the birth of this book in its current form, who listened to and offered valuable insight on the first chapters as they moved from rough draft to polished manuscript, and who sent good wishes into the air from the 30th floor; Zita Christian, who provided words of wisdom and moments of magic, and who challenged me to be big; Louise Temple who role models the spiritual power of words; and all the other writing sisters of heart who made this possible just by being—Emily Hanlon, Susan Omilian, Judy Adourian, Marj Hahne, Ann Walradt, Marsha Browne, Nina Reimer, Dorothy Randall Gray and Diane Gallo, with a special thank you to Hannelore Hahn for giving birth to the Guild, and to her daughter, Elizabeth Julia for her help in sustaining it.

Other guides and helpers along the way include Alex Moore at *ForeWord Magazine*, Mary Jo Zazueta, who designed the cover and formatted the book, Loren Beller who cleared the muddy waters and help me be a big fish, Nancy L. Butler-Ross, the bookmuse, and Sherri Rosen, my publicist.

Weaving a life is always a family affair and so I am especially grateful to the aunts and grandmother who taught me needle arts—Grace, Franny, and Reva—as well as my parents, Paul and Pat, and my stepmother, Gail.

And while this is a book for women, I could not have written it without the many lessons I learned at the loom while parenting three miraculous, marvelous, multi-talented sons, Stephen, Christopher, and Jason. I watch with delight and awe as they weave their own lives of beauty and love. Of course, they have the best of examples in the miracle that is my husband, Bob.

Introduction

May the warp be the white light of morning,
May the weft be the red light of evening,
May the fringes be the falling rain,
May the border be the standing rainbow,
Thus weave for us a garment of brightness.

~ SONG OF THE SKY LOOM (TEWA)

WEAVING IS ONE OF THE OLDEST CRAFTS, dating back to the Neolithic period, thousands of years before knitting was invented. Weaving was the first way humans found to clothe themselves with something other than skins and furs.

Weaving, or woven fabric, touches you, literally, every day. Like that advertising slogan, it is "the fabric of your life." The towels you use to dry yourself after your morning shower are woven. The white linen blouse or oxford shirt you put on for work is woven. The jeans you slip on in the evening to relax, the sheets you lie down on at night to sleep, the fabric of your sofa, chair seats, drapes, kitchen towels, and rugs are all woven.

Whether we realize it consciously or unconsciously, because of its antiquity, weaving not only permeates our lives, it also permeates our language. How many times have you used the phrase "woven together", or "weaves through" to imply an integration of elements? How about that familiar warning—

"Oh what a tangled web we weave when first we practice to deceive." Even the word we use for our internet community, the "Web" refers both to the web of fabric and to the web spun by a spider, an arachnid which gets its name from a mythical mortal, Arachne, who dared to challenge the goddess of weaving, Athena, to a contest. Challenging a goddess is never a good idea and Arachne was turned into a spider for her pride.

Weaving is primal, basic, calling to us from the beginnings of civilization.

Weaving is also magical. In its basic structure of vertical threads crossing over and under horizontal threads, creating thousands of tiny crosses in any fabric, weaving incorporates the numinous energy of both the masculine and feminine, the physical and spiritual, the primal and divine creative forces.

In those tiny crosses are represented the religions and spiritual traditions of the world, such as the Christian cross, the Celtic cross, the pagan cross, the Egyptian ankh, the Druidic Tree of Life, Native American traditions' honoring of the four directions, and others.

When I began weaving in the early 80's, I did not understand or appreciate what magic this craft held or what it could teach me on a personal and spiritual level. I must have been pulled, though, to that first weaving class by a distant memory of one of my favorite childhood Disney movies, *The Three Lives of Thomasina*. The movie takes place in early 20th century Wales and has all the makings of a fairytale. One of the central characters played by Susan Hampshire lives in a cottage in the woods. All the local children think this woman is a witch because of the strange, rhythmic sounds coming from her cottage. What they discover instead is a blue-eyed, ethereal, blonde woman sitting at a large floor loom weaving away. The suspicious thumping sound is only the beat of the reed against the cloth.

That image must have brewed in my creative soul for many years, for when the chance came to learn weaving, I took it. Several years later, when woven items accumulated about the house, I sold my work, first through the local guild, then at craft shows.

About the same time I learned to weave and thus grow a career, I also started on a conscious spiritual journey, exploring feminist theology, Wicca, Native American spiritual traditions (I am a small part Cherokee on my mother's side), Hinduism, Buddhism, meditation, and yoga. On the journey, I kept looking for "the Teacher." I kept hearing over and over in my mind, "When the student is ready the teacher will appear."

So, when the teacher didn't appear, I asked myself, *aren't I ready yet?* What I discovered is that frequently the teacher doesn't come in the form of a guru or a wise sage. Often the teacher is a relationship with someone—a boss, a partner, a child, a friend, or even a pet. The teacher can also be a practice —the doing of something with commitment, consistency, focus, and endurance. In my case, weaving is one of my primary spiritual teachers—it just took me a while to realize it.

The other thing it took me some time to realize is that weaving is not something separate from all the other things I do as wife, mother, writer, creativity coach and dreamworker. For years, I asked myself, Is this what I am supposed to do? Or am I supposed to be a writer, or a teacher or, or, or.. Gradually, I understood that weaving nourishes and adds dimension to all the other parts of my life and that other parts of my life give understanding and dimension to my weaving. Weaving taught me patience, letting go, staying in the moment and acceptance, as well as other insights. In fact, everything I did was—excuse the expression—*interwoven*!

While I may still have a way to travel to enlightenment, at least now I know I merely have to follow the threads of a craft that stretches forward and backward in time, that joins the material with the spiritual, and I am well on my way.

In centuries past, if someone wanted to learn a craft, they first paid a master craftsman for an apprenticeship. Under the auspices and guidance of that accomplished weaver, the apprentice would learn the skills and techniques necessary to practice the craft. If the apprentice was interested and a good student, the master weaver would also teach some of the tricks and secrets of the craft that were learned after years of work. Eventually, the apprentice would acquire all the knowledge and skills necessary to become a full member of the craft guild and eventually set up her own studio.

I wrote this book because, although I may not call myself a master weaver in the technical sense, on a spiritual level there are many things I have learned that I hope will be of help to you. Maybe, here in these pages, you will find a few words or ideas that show you how to weave more color or texture into your life, how to find the threads, the rhythm, the balance to weave a life of compassion, creativity, and spirituality. By understanding the power of the choices you make each day, of the importance of using quality tools, physical and spiritual, and developing the ability to stay flexible and creative, you will discover that you can be an adept and practiced weaver of your own life.

HOW TO USE THIS BOOK

Every craft and profession has its own particular language or group of terms. Weaving is no exception. Though many of the terms like weave, loom, warp, and weft, show up frequently in our daily conversation, we often are using them outside the context of the craft and therefore understand them differently. So that you will understand what I mean when I use the terms, and in case you are not familiar with them at all, there is a section at the end of the book called "Language of the Loom." Terms like warp and weft and shuttle are described in, what I hope, are clear and easy definitions. A labeled illustration of the loom is also included. You may wish to read this section first to familiarize yourself with the language, or, if you have some sense of the terms, flip back to it as you read to clarify any particular term for you.

At the end of each chapter is a section called Thrums. In weaving, thrums are the ends of the warp threads that are left hanging from the back of the loom once the woven fabric is finished and cut off. Some weavers throw those ends away. Some use them to make tassels, or hair for fabric dolls, or filler for pillows. Some weavers weave those thrums back into other weavings.

The thrums in this book come at the end of my weaving of each chapter. They are questions and suggested actions for you to ponder, write about, or act on, that may help you integrate what you have just read. You as the reader and the weaver of your own life have the same options as other weavers. You may ignore, in a sense, throw away these thrums. Or, you can take time to think about them and write answers to them, and follow through with some of the suggested actions, thereby weaving them into your life. Or you can use them as starting points for new questions and actions, thus creating entirely new work with them, an adornment for your weaving.

All of those options are useful and appropriate. You are the weaver, so there are no wrong choices. I am here to show you the steps and secrets I know to weave a woman's life—what has worked for me. My wish is that what I share here with you leads you to discover your own secrets of the craft, and to weave a life of beauty, wisdom, and love.

Today She Weaves a Blue Scarf
by Leslie McIlroy

Weaving is a woman's work,
the delicate warp and fiber.
She alone finds the pattern
that entwines marriage and meter,
debts and babies, shadows
and art—the lonely nights
wound with colors of her heart stretched long
across the looming darkness.

She weaves and she drinks.
She weaves and she dreams.
She weaves and she weeps.
She weaves.

And sometimes she runs the yarn
through her fingers, imagining
what follows, but never pretending
to know, for the next weft might
be rich and raddled in a way
only time can fabricate—the close
fit of a sweater worn thin. She lets
the threads fall to the floor
and find their way into
the cloth, she lets her weight
shift to accommodate the reach
and pull. She lets her mind
slip into the rhythm of light,
the rhythm of invention,
the rhythm of desire.

She weaves and she drinks.
She weaves and she dreams.
She weaves and she weeps.
She weaves.

And "magic" is the word
she uses to describe that moment
when the last knot is tied—
when she tries herself on—
when she selects a new frame,
a new color, a new texture,
to begin once again,
the tapestry of her life.

Weaving
a
Woman's Life

Lesson One

QUALITY TOOLS—
PHYSICAL AND SPIRITUAL

"My diary seems to keep me whole."
~ ANAIS NIN

"I've dreamt in my life dreams that have stayed with me ever after, and
changed my ideas: they've gone through and through me, like wine
through water, and altered the color of my mind."
~ EMILY BRONTE

"Ritual is the act of sanctifying action—even ordinary actions—
so that it has meaning ..."
~ CHRISTINA BALDWIN

THE SEDUCTIVELY SILKY TEXTURE AND CURVES OF A finely crafted piece of wood furniture appeals to my sensual self. So each time I chose and purchased one of my looms, it was because I was seduced by the wood frame's buttery light color and the satiny smooth feel of the breast (front) beam under my hand. Yes, the facts that the harnesses moved quietly up and down, and that the frame did not wiggle and rattle, were also important but not any more so than the beauty of the loom itself. Rubbing my hand along the breast beam of any of my four looms is as satisfying as brushing my hand across my woven chenille scarves. My tools need to meet both criteria—aesthetics and function.

Recently, I realized what a difference quality tools make when my husband and I bought a new set of fine stainless steel cookware. These replaced the so-so set of stainless cookware we had received as a wedding gift thirty years ago. Though I built my skills as a cook using those first pans, once I used the new pans, my pleasure in their sparkling surfaces and the way they sat solidly on the cook top, and, even more importantly, the way they heated evenly and cleaned easily, brought forth an intuitive creativity in my cooking. My husband was treated to night after night of new ways of preparing chicken, lamb, and pasta.

I respond to my weaving tools in the same way—if they work well, look beautiful, and are pleasing to touch, then weaving is a pleasure. Occasionally, I forget what an effect this has on my work. Right now I have a fly shuttle (that boat-shaped wooden tool that carries the bobbin wound with weft thread back and forth) whose shaft does not hold the bobbin firmly in place. This requires me to fuss with it each time I change the bobbin and slows me down. Those shuttles cost around $80 a piece, so making do for a while made some sense, but I have been making do for years. It is time for a new shuttle.

The spiritual tools we use for weaving our life are even more important and highly individualistic. The tools below help me to find direction, perspective, inspiration, and guidance through all aspects of my life. Indeed, my dreams and my journals kept me moving forward through the days of grieving after my mother died, and through the challenges of being a mother of three active, intelligent boys. These tools were my anchor to sanity and my hope for healing.

2

I hope you will use them—and that, with them, you will weave your life with more clarity, confidence, and creativity.

THE JOURNAL

I grew up at a time when a girl was given a diary almost as soon as she was old enough to write. My mother gave me my first diary. It had a soft vinyl, pale blue cover and lined pages inside. I remember the magic of opening it and thinking how special it was to have a place to record my thoughts and actions of the day. At that time, my biggest secret was who I had a crush on. Even when my maternal Great-aunt Linda gave me a leather-bound, gold-leaf diary with a lock and key, which made me feel very grown-up, the most important thing in it was still my current crush!

Later, when I entered college and the period of life for testing and defining who I was, the diary—or journal—became a place not only to talk about the boy I was in love with (who was to become my husband) but also to record my thoughts about sex, drugs, and my relationships with dorm mates and others. My understanding of the purpose for keeping a journal stretched.

As a writer and lover of words, recording the events of my life was just another way of telling story as I moved through those college years, falling in love and then marrying. Then three things happened almost at the same point in my life: I remembered and recorded my dreams; I recorded my thoughts about weaving and writing; and my mother was diagnosed with breast cancer.

At that point in time, my husband and I had recently moved out into the country after giving birth to our third son. Our house was surrounded by marsh and woods, and the closest neighbor was about half a mile down the road. I stayed home with our three young boys while my husband, Bob, made the 40-minute drive each day into work in Albany. In my isolation, the journal became my friend with the sympathetic, never-tiring, never-judgmental ear.

Daily, I was challenged to find a way to balance the needs of three young boys with my own desire to develop a career of weaving and writing, and the worries about my mother who fought with breast cancer for her life.

The more I wrote in my journal about my life and my dreams, which were vivid and frequent, the more perspective, patience, and insight into big and small moments I gained through them. So I read books on keeping a journal. One of my favorites then and now is Christina Baldwin's *Journal as a Life Companion*. In her book, I discovered how much keeping a

3

journal could offer me, especially as a companion on my spiritual journey, recording not just what happened but my responses and understandings about events and people. From her book, I learned about timed writing (usually five to seven minutes) and flow writing (stream of consciousness), about writing in the journal as ritual, and about the power of the journal for moving toward forgiveness and through grief. Illustrated by one of my favorite artists, Susan Sedon Boulet, the book gave me tools for recording and understanding my life's journey from a spiritual perspective.

Throughout the first years of living in a farmhouse we heated with only a woodstove while temperatures outside dropped to a minus 60 wind chill factor, and the boys came down with one virus after another; through my mother's illness and death; through recurring bouts of frustration and helplessness; and through dream after dream, the journal took it all in—patiently and silently—no matter how whiney I became, or how sad.

Forget diamonds, her journal is a girl's best friend. In today's world of constantly changing jobs, communities, and even family units, the journal is a reliable and ever-present friend that can hold up a mirror to who we are at any place in time, reflecting back to us successes, failures, and patterns of behavior and emotions. Journals are a great place to vent anger, hurt, and especially grief. After my mother died, I missed our weekly Saturday phone calls, so I used my journal as a place to write weekly letters to her to bridge the distance between life and death. Those letters helped ease the pain of my loss.

Journals are the place to weave the dreams of the future, dreams that are yet too tenuous and fragile to be spoken aloud. Writing down hopes and dreams for family, relationships, career, or your spiritual journey is the first step in manifesting and weaving them into your life. Sometimes words are not enough to empower the dreams or visions, so recording pictures of them in the journal by drawing or creating small collages of images cut from magazines, newspapers, and cards helps to clarify and strengthen those dreams. Your journal is also a good place to work out how you will weave these dreams weft by weft. And it is here that you can note and complain about the knots and snarls that challenge you along the way, and your failures or successes in untangling them.

As with any tool, find a journal that is both functional and appealing to your senses. You may prefer a black and white speckled notebook that brings back happy memories of school days, or, at the other extreme, a luxuriously bound leather journal. Consider whether you want something large enough to give you room for pasting and drawing pictures, or whether you want something small and precious that fits easily in your hand.

Bookstores now offer and sell all kinds of journals, some with prompts or quotations, some with pockets for collecting memorabilia, and others with colorful covers that honor the imaginative life recorded inside. I have purchased small, leather bound journals for my life, journals with illustrated covers by one of my favorite artists, Kinuko Y. Craft, for my writing projects, and designed and created my own special dream journal.

In addition to choosing a pleasing journal, make sure your writing tool fits well in the hand and moves ink easily onto the page. Again, this is an individual preference that ranges from the inexpensive ballpoint pen to the classical fountain pen. For those who illustrate their journals, a small selection of colored pencils, markers, and pastels are important. I like to browse hobby, stationery, and even college bookstores for the writing tool that makes me happy. I particularly like pens with purple ink.

And please don't let the old diary dictum of writing in your journal every day prevent you from keeping a journal. As with a friend, you choose the times to be together sharing your life. If a day or two, a week or two, even a month or two goes by, don't fret, feel guilty, and stop. Just know that this particular friend is very forgiving and waits patiently for your return.

5

DREAMS

I have been an active dreamer from the age of five or six. In fact, I still remember dreams from that period in my life, so vivid and emotionally powerful were they. One dream involved my father and a tiger that was loose in our small farming town. Years later, as an adult accomplished in dreamwork, I related the dream to my father only to discover that he used to have dreams about a tiger attacking him!

Dreams have led me to new directions in my work. One dream involved my walking into a gallery and seeing the director bent over a doubleweave framed weaving. When I asked who the weaver was, the director said my name. I remembered the dream when I awoke and within the next month wove two pieces similar to the dream weaving. A photograph of one of the weavings, Mediated Transcendance, was used for the cover of a book!

After my mother died, I dreamt of her sitting and rocking in a chair in a small moving van. My siblings moved in and out of the truck without seeing her even though I kept telling them she was there. My mom looked at me. "You are the only one who can see me," she said. After sharing that dream with my father, I discovered that a friend of my mom's from church had a similar dream, this one taking place in her church—none of the other parishioners could see Mom, only Ann. I had other dreams where Mom came to visit and reassure me.

6

I dreamt about our middle son, Chris, having a party in our house without asking us. I didn't pay attention to it. My husband and I went away for a weekend craft show where I exhibited and sold my weavings and came home to find things looking fairly normal. Then I noticed a cigarette stub in our yard, a beer bottle cap in our family room rug! When questioned, Chris admitted to having a small get together for friends that grew a little beyond his expectations. The dream had warned me and I hadn't listened!

If you don't remember, record, and work with your sleep dreams, you may miss out on a significant source of information, guidance, and inspiration for the weaving of your life.

Whatever your religious or spiritual background, there is usually a dreaming tradition found within it. The role of dreaming in our lives is as basic as sleeping and as important. Scientific studies show that when a person is deprived of the opportunity to dream they can become ill both physically and psychologically.

Dreams are an important tool to see the whole web of our life, not one little corner of it. They can give us guidance for living our life from day to day. The Iroquois believe that we dream everything before it happens (perhaps the source of those feelings of déjà vu we often encounter). If so, then paying attention to them could help us make better choices and avoid the actions that lead to more problems instead of solutions.

Take time to remember and record your dreams. You might want to keep a separate journal for your dreams or simply partition off a portion of your regular journal for dreams alone. If, at first, you don't remember your dreams, then begin with whatever you do remember, even if it is only a song or phrase that keeps repeating itself in your head when you wake up in the morning. That phrase could be the key into what you were dreaming about earlier. Or record whatever you are feeling, or whatever thought pops into your head upon awakening. By getting into the practice of recording something in the morning, you train your brain and alert your dream self that you want to, and are ready, to remember and work with your dreams.

7

When you wake with a dream you remember, record it in your journal. First, date and title your dream for future refer- ence. Then record the dream or fragment in present tense. Even if you do nothing more than this, you derive surprising benefits. First, you will discern patterns not only in your dreaming but when placed against the background of what is going on in your life, patterns in your life as well. I had students share dreams that have a common theme repeating themselves with variations over a period of time, such as wedding dreams, or going to school dreams, and they indicate a theme, emotion, or event recurring in their life as well.

Secondly, just by paying attention to your dreams, you'll remember them with more frequency. In fact, you may get to a point where you need to ask your dream self for a night off—too much dream remembering can be exhausting!

Thirdly, you may have dreams that clue you in to when to call or reach out to friends and family, or alert you to when they will be in touch with you.

And, you may find that just by remembering and recording your dreams, they give you more and more information on your daily life.

For those of us whose time and budgets do not allow for the ideal vacation, our dreams can even be a great way to get away for awhile, to live on an island, fly like a bird, or be queen for the night. If nothing else, they will entertain and inspire you.

So, when you go to bed tonight, write down on a piece of paper, " I want to be aware of and remember my dreams in the morning so I may record them." Place it beneath your pillow and see what happens. When you wake, give the dream, dream fragment, or even feeling, a title such as "Broken Tea Set" or "Journey to the Moon" or "Hoping for an Exit Visa". Record the dream in present tense, noting how the dream makes you feel.

Do you see any similarities between the dream and waking reality? For example, does the house, or car, or woman in the dream look like your house or car or friend in waking reality, or is it unlike anything you know or have seen? Is there an animal, person, place, or object that draws your attention in the dream? Have a dialogue with that object or person, writing your questions with one hand and the object's answers with the other. The reason for using the non-dominant hand in the dialogue is to access the part of the brain you normally don't use for writing. For most people it is the left hand that is non-dominant. Using it accesses the right brain. Even if you are left-handed and use your right hand to dialogue, you are breaking through ingrained behavior and responses, which again, lets you access new ways of understanding or perceiving.

If, as with some of my friends, you can't use the other hand, then at least use different colored pens for the dialogue and see what happens.

Remember, be patient with the process. If you have not been remembering or working with your dreams, it make take several nights or even weeks of reminding your dream self that you want to make contact for that message to get through.

RITUALS

Though we sometimes use the words interchangeably, a routine can be ritualized, but a ritual, our next tool, should not become routine.

Upon entering my studio, before I sat down to write this, I put on beautiful music and lit a stick of incense. This small ritual signals to me that I am here to give meaning and significance to what I am about to do, and that I am to do it with awareness. This ritual separates what I do in my studio from what I do outside it and moves me into a quiet, receptive, creative state of mind and being.

A ritual is different from a routine in that, though there may be a pattern of actions repeated, the purpose of the pattern in a ritual is to bring a mindfulness to the moment and, as in the case of spiritual or religious ritual, to help us transcend from the ordinary into the extraordinary. Rituals, big and small, make up an important and significant part of our life whether we recognize them or not.

9

Bedtime in our house when the boys were little was not a routine, though it followed a pattern, but a ritual—a preparation for moving into the realm of sleep and dreams. This ritual occurred at a set time each night and had certain steps to it. First came the reading of a story by their father or me, then the donning of pajamas, then the brushing of teeth, followed by the climb into bed where each of the three boys was carefully tucked in. Then came the four nursery rhymes sung by whichever parent was performing the ritual, and then a kiss goodnight on each forehead, and one last hug.

This was not a routine but a ritual, because it was done with awareness and focused attention on our sons. Their father and I served as their guides and escorts into the land of Nod. With rare exceptions, this ritual was enacted even when we were traveling or had guests, and we believe that this ritual, done with focused awareness on our sons, is the reason we never had any problems with the boys about bedtime or going to sleep.

Rituals provide a structure to our day and a rhythm (another important element of weaving). Rituals are an intrinsic part of being human.

I saw in my three sons that the structures of ritual, whether for going to bed or celebrating the holidays, made them more relaxed, more stable, more certain about the world around them. In fact, when my husband or I tried to veer from the ritual, such as forgetting a song in our medley of bedtime nursery rhymes, the oversight was quickly brought to our attention. Even now, years later, when our sons are grown men, they enjoy certain repeated rituals around the holidays. These rituals serve to set those days apart from the rest of the year and help them feel rooted and truly at home.

Rituals also act as a bridge. In its more sacred context, ritual acts to transport us from the physical to the transcendent and back again. When you walk through the door of the church, synagogue, or temple, acts such as removing shoes, blessing and crossing with holy water, or even just the quieting of voice and motion, are the small ritual signals to ourselves and others that we are moving into sacred space and time.

With our increasingly busy lives, rituals can offer a way to signal our minds and bodies to let go, to leave the stresses of the day at the office, with the kids, on the phone, in the car, behind. Too often we rush from our beds in the morning into the day, home again and back into bed in one long blur that never draws the line between work and relaxation, between doing and being. Creating rituals that mark transitions in the day can help us slow down, draw a deep breath, and let go of our worries.

Quality Tools

What if, after slipping the shoes from our feet and check-
ing the mail, we sat down for five or ten minutes with a cup of
tea or coffee and just gazed out a window or listened to a lovely
piece of music, remembering to breathe deeply—a small ritual
of homecoming? Since we are probably beyond the age when
someone will rock us and sing us to sleep (though some of us
have partners who read to us before bed), we may need to create
small bedtime rituals that require more than face cream and
toothbrush. As women, though we are great at creating routines that increase efficiency, we too often become dulled by the
very routines that help us move through the day. To transform
routine into ritual, consider lighting a candle before a bath,
playing some dirty dancing music while cleaning the house, or
lighting incense before lovemaking. Small actions like these can
bring a new awareness to the moment so that taking a bath,
cleaning the house, and making love become acts of blessing
and renewal.

THRUMS
  . . . *the leftover threads at the end of the warp and what to do
with them* . . .

11

- ❧ Look at the tools you use each day to care for your
  space, cook your meals, help you in your work, assist
  you in your creative play. Are they quality tools? Do
  they please you when you hold them or work with
  them? Or do they need to be mended? Have they worn
  out? Pick one tool that is not as beautiful as it is functional and look at a way to make it more pleasing or at
  the possibility of replacing it. Then track the difference
  that changed tool makes in that task.

- ❧ Find a journal specifically pleasing to you to be your
  silent friend and a comfortable or smooth-writing pen
  especially for recording your life. Sit in front of a
  mirror and observe what you see there. Who are you at

this point in time? What badges of honor from your life do you see in the mirror? What hopes and dreams do you see offered to you? Give yourself at least ten minutes to write the answers to these questions in your new journal.

❧ Choose either a separate journal or a place in your regular journal to record your dreams. Close your eyes and think of a dream that you remember, either from long ago or just last night. Follow the process for recording a title, the dream, and the feelings. Does the dream provide any understandings about yesterday's events? Does the dream offer warnings or insights for the day ahead? Record your dreams for several weeks and observe if there are any common themes or patterns, like weddings, or water, or losing your purse.

❧ Make note of where rituals in your life have lost their significance and become routine. Create and practice new rituals for moving from sleep into your day, or for letting go of the day's stresses to smooth your path into the evening and sleep. Choose an action you can take to signal to yourself that you are moving into a different state of mind, an awareness of the moment, such as lighting a candle, burning incense, or putting on a certain type of music. Record in your journal over several weeks any changes the rituals trigger, such as feeling more relaxed in the evening, or noticing more around you during the day, or functioning more cheerfully at work.

12

Lesson Two

SILENCE AND SOLITUDE—
THE SPACE BETWEEN THE THREADS

"What a commentary on our civilization, when being alone is considered
suspect; when one has to apologize for it, make excuses, hide the fact
that one practices it—like some secret vice."
~ ANNE MORROW LINDBERGH

"If there is one consistent thing that stops people committed to doing
creative work from doing it, it is this: a lack of necessary silence in their
lives, an inability or unwillingness to find and stay with the stillness, to
regularly create empty time in their day or their week."
~ ORIAH MOUTAIN DREAMER

TO WEAVE THE FABRIC OF A LIFE WITH WISDOM AND
creativity, silence and solitude are absolute necessi-
ties. Generation and gestation occur more easily in
silence and solitude. In the rich soil of silence and solitude, new
ideas, thoughts, and even guidance can sprout up, flowering
along with solutions to challenges and concerns.

I live in the country in the foothills of the Catskills, a place
some would call "the back of beyond." In truth, it is not as isolated as it could be if I lived in the wilds of Wyoming but for
many people it is really "out there."

The isolation, though, is what I love because in the isolation
resides the silence and solitude that living in the country, at least
half a mile from any neighbor, provides. I love sitting at the

loom with the windows open, listening to the birds singing their territorial boundaries while I throw shuttle back and forth. So I was thrown off balance when, several years ago a woman bought the property around us and moved into a modular home on one side of us, then helped her son and his wife and their two sons move into the same style modular home in back of us. Suddenly we went from isolated country living to a strange kind of rural suburb!

After not seeing or hearing anyone around us for 20 years, the sense of intrusion was overwhelming. By the end of the fall my husband and I had planted six pine trees on our property line that adjoined the new neighbor's so that in five to ten years we could not see her home. But insult was added to injury the first day in early spring when we heard the annoyingly loud buzzing and revving of her two grandsons' ATV's. What had been a creative silence broken only by the sweet song of bird, cricket, or frog (and the occasional passing car), now became an irritating vibration on ear and spirit every time I opened a window or stepped outside.

I worried about what the noise might do to the birds that lived in the neighborhood—the owls, the hawks, the herons, the grosbeaks, and the orioles. After all, if the noise upset my system, how could it not upset theirs? Fortunately, they proved to be hardy souls, and after the first summer, the novelty for the two boys of driving the machines up and down the dirt road for the short distance between their house and the end of the road wore off.

What interested me was how much I had taken the silence— or the naturally noisy silence—for granted. From the spring call of the peepers to the hooting of the great horned owl to the howling of coyotes, I love it all. This symphony of nature calms me, slows me down, makes space for reflection and renewal. It is the lullaby to my own creative process. And like primitive man and woman before me, I sense that as long as the birds are singing and the crickets chirping, all must be right with my world—no predator is creeping up on me planning its dinner!

Silence is important to the health of our nervous systems. Were you ever in a hospital nursery or around a newborn baby? Any sudden loud noise triggers the infant's startle reflex. The baby's arms and legs thrust out as if to push away the offending noise, the eyes go wide to take in the impending danger, and the infant often wails an alert.

Our arms and legs may not go into contortions, but the constant barrage of noise from our vehicles, appliances, entertainment, and computers definitely affects our nervous system. Studies have shown that continuous noise assault can cause nausea, headaches, sleeplessness, and decreased sex drive.

Whether sitting in a restaurant, riding an elevator, or walking through a shopping mall, we are forced to listen to someone else's idea of music (always much too loud), as if we would be unable to enjoy ourselves without this background noise. Silence seems an anathema to our society.

Of course, we can't put all the blame on public places. When was the last time you were willing to be in your car or home or office without some background companion of talk radio, music, or TV chatter? As a society, we have lost the ability to be in silence. Is it because in silence we might actually begin to hear our own thoughts, feel our feelings, and, most frighteningly for some of us, even discover we are alone?

15

Being alone, solitude, and being lonely, or loneliness, are not necessarily the same state. Solitude implies a chosen state of aloneness, while loneliness is something thrust on us. The ability to seek out, appreciate, and enjoy solitude is almost as lost an art in our culture as silence. We shrink from solitude because we fear that, while being alone and listening to our thoughts in the silence, we might also discover that we are lonely.

Yet, if we give ourselves the gift of solitude, we also gain the gift of freedom from outside demands, if only temporarily.

These days of busy careers balanced with raising children while also trying to stay fit, young and beautiful and be a Martha Stewart clone, pulls us into an unending stream of expectations, demands, wants and needs from family, friends, neighbors, and your ever present telemarketer. Think about how many times a day your attention is requested, nay, demanded and fractured! Watch me, mommy! Listen to me! Pay attention to this! Buy this! Try this! Help me! On and on and on the voices—and the noise—go.

And where in that clamor of voices is the still, small voice of me? How will I ever hear my inner voice, let alone my outer voice, if I never separate from the clamor of other voices?

I am sure an advanced yogi might be able to shut out, turn off, the clamor—although I would like to see him take on a persistent three-year-old—but most of us are daily worn down by the never ending clamor for our focus and response.

Most cultures had and have a way of honoring the retreat into silence and solitude—the vision quest of Native American cultures and the monastic retreats of Christian traditions, for example. For women, that time of retreat into silence and solitude came monthly with menstrual cycles and a retreat into the red tent or the moon lodge. Since our culture no longer honors time away, we must as women find ways to enter into silence and solitude.

Often I weave in silence because this creates a meditative space. While the reed beats against the warp, back and forth, back and forth, and the treadles lift and drop harnesses, up and down, up and down, creating it's own kind of syncopated music, my mind has room to roam, to think thoughts otherwise crammed out of my head by the many demands of the days and weeks. Yes, I may consider what needs to be done when I step from the studio, but I may also think about my newest idea for a story, or how I feel about a son moving away, or what I would like to plant in the garden. Often, I am happy just to hear the wind chimes, the fountain, or the song of birds outside the studio windows. Weaving in silence becomes meditation. Like beads on a rosary, each thread threaded through the heddle, each pass of the shuttle through the warp is like another prayer bead clicked through in my litany.

In that rhythmic silence and solitude, I am renewed and refreshed.

THRUMS

- ❧ Spend one day being aware of all the places mechanical noises occur. Can any of them be reduced in time or volume?

- ❧ Make note of all the times you choose distraction over silence and solitude by playing background music or turning the TV on even when you are not watching it.

- ❧ When was the last time you chose or were able to spend time alone—on a walk, sitting on your porch, on the beach, or curled up in a comfortable chair watching the world out your window? Can you make room in your schedule for at least ten minutes alone each day to practice solitude, to hear the silence, to hear your own inner voice bubble up to the surface of your consciousness? What do you hear? Record it in your journal.

- ❧ Also record in your journal what feelings come up for you when you think about *choosing* to be alone. Where and when would it be luxurious, even fun, to be alone—at the beach, on a walk through the woods, at home when your husband is away on business and your schedule is your own?

17

Lesson Three

TIME AND SPACE— MAKING ROOM FOR WHO WE ARE

"There is an endless net of threads throughout the universe.
The horizontal threads are in space.
The vertical threads are in time.

At every crossing of the threads,
there is an individual."
~ THE RIG VEDA

LONG AGO, WHEN WOMEN'S BODIES WERE MORE in tune with nature, time was the thread that wove together the passing of the seasons, the waxing and waning of the moon, with the changes and ageing of a woman's body. In fact, in most cultures the words for moon, menstruation, and time, have common roots, stemming from the fact that timekeeping began with women's marking of their menstrual cycles and pregnancies. Each month, with the waning of the moon, menstruating women used that time to remove themselves from the daily life of the community and the never-ending tasks of care giving and nurturing, to sit, rest, and recuperate; to be quiet or to share stories with other women, to give up daily demands while their body released old life and prepared for new. This time of rest was the first "Sabbat", honoring the menstruation of the Goddess.

Very few of us practice a Sabbat of any kind nowadays,

19

with the exception of those still actively involved in a church or temple. Even then, the Sabat is often nothing more than the hour or two spent in church; and no sooner do the temple doors close behind us than life resumes its pace.

Wouldn't it be nice if every month, instead of swallowing doses of Midol and plowing ahead with our busy schedules, we could remove ourselves to our equivalent of a tepee or tent, and sit meditating, reading, weaving a basket, writing, or just sleeping? Five days later, we could then emerge and, like our wombs and the moon, be rested and renewed?

Given the world we live in today, unless we move to the back of beyond, our chances for retreat and renewal on a monthly, even yearly, basis are slim. Even when we do manage to schedule time away on vacation, these trips are over-planned, often rushed, and frequently accompanied by our cell phones and laptops. So how *can* we afford to carve out time for ourselves?

Perhaps the real question is how can we afford *not* to? After all, if we give all of our time and energy away to others without time for ourselves, soon the time we give away has no energy or value with it, and worse, may carry an underlying resentment. How many times have you or some friend or other woman in your life bemoaned the lack of time to accomplish all the tasks and responsibilities lining up on that infamous to-do list? Yet we will then turn around and volunteer for some new committee.

What is worse is that we sabotage ourselves by buying into the newest cultural myth of woman as super-multitasker. We are so accomplished at multitasking, that to stop all our doing for others to do for ourselves carries with it the double whammy of finding the time and then suppressing unwarranted guilt when we do. Instead, we make our lists, toss those balls in the air, and start juggling everyone else's priorities.

Did you know that multitasking, rather than deeming you a superwoman, actually makes you stupid? Recent studies from universities and the National Institute of Mental Health show that trying to do several things at once can actually take longer and reduce the brainpower available for each task! Intense multitasking can create a stress response that damages cells that form new memory. So when was the last time you dialed the phone while cleaning up after dinner and sorting through the mail, only to wonder frantically when you hear the first rings, who it is you called?

Do you find yourself driving to work, stopping to drop off the kids at school and day care, while making lists in your mind of things to do on the way home, while also dialing the pediatrician's number to make an appointment for your youngest child's check-up? Do you find yourself, like me, trying to make dinner, bake cookies, go through mail, and do a load of laundry, and then feeling, when you finally fall into bed, that you may be exhausted but, boy, did you get a lot done!

But what did you get done? In that list of things accomplished today, and that list of things to do tomorrow, where is there an item that says "time for self" or "time for my creativity" or, " time to relax"?

As wonderful as the rise in popularity of handwork is, especially knitting, with stars like Julia Roberts and Cameron Diaz taking up the needles, we have to ask ourselves, "Am I doing this to slow down, to be with myself, and my desire to create or am I using this to avoid guilt about 'wasted' time?"

With few exceptions, weaving is not portable. I can't take the loom, however small, to the doctor's office. There is no multitasking with weaving. One of the first things weaving teaches about time is that doing one thing at a time and doing it well is enough. I am sitting at the loom or I am not. And when I am weaving I must pay attention to which treadles I am pushing down, and how the weft is arcing through the warp before it is beaten into place. The only thing I can do in addition to winding warp, threading the loom, or throwing the shuttle is to listen to CD's. I must be present with the process. Weaving has its own pace and forces me to slow down my body, my breath, and my mind.

21

Another thing weaving teaches about time is its forward movement. Weaving has a first this, then that, structure to it. First I wind the warp, then I dress and thread the loom, then I weave that warp, then I remove the woven warp and finish the fabric. I cannot skip steps. I cannot weave until I dress the loom. I cannot dress the loom until I wind the warp. This linear movement creates a directional focus, dispelling scattered thinking. Studies on multitasking show that tasks taken one at a time (do this, then that) are done more efficiently and more effectively when we place our full focus on what we are doing, systematically following the steps necessary to complete the project.

So I must weave the warp as it unwinds before me, just as the minutes and hours and days of my life unwind before me. It does no good for me to wish to hurry the process. I can only move ahead one row of weft at a time, one breath at a time. To be at the loom is to be present in the moment. And being present in the moment, allows me to decide how to spend each moment, to determine what my priorities for that time are. Once spent they cannot be recovered.

The challenge for us as women is to find time and courage to silence the voices and ignore the needs clamoring for our attention; a time where we can stop, however briefly, trying to be super multitasker and give our full attention to just one thing we *want* to do for ourselves. Whether that one thing is to knit, weave, paint, read, walk, or nap, to give ourselves to it completely is both a luxury and a necessity. So how do we do that?

Many years ago, while working on my MFA, I had two sons who were just past toddlerhood. I spent every day, all day with them, supervising their play, taking them to story hour at the library, running them to doctors' appointments. Finding time, especially uninterrupted time, for the reading, writing and weaving I needed to do was a challenge. I often wrote in the evenings when my husband, Bob, was home and available to the boys, but just as often, I fell asleep over paper and pen, exhausted by my day with the dynamic duo. My one special productive time each week came on Saturday when Bob loaded the two boys into their car seats for a drive to the grocery store. This little outing for father and sons gave me a precious hour and a half to myself. The door closed behind chirping voices and I breathed deep of the silence and the space and the time, before I sat down to read or write.

A neighbor down the street was working on her PhD and had two small children as well. Her solution to finding time for herself and her work was to go to bed at night at the same time as the children and then rise at 4 a.m. to work for several hours in the uninterrupted peace and quiet.

Friends of mine who were stay-at-home moms organized a playgroup for their young children. Once a week one mother took her turn minding the children while the other mothers did what they wanted to do. One mother painted, another went shopping, another wrote. Whatever they chose to do, it was time for them.

Make time for yourself a priority. Declare it to yourself and to others around you. For peace of mind, for clarity of mind and self, we need time for solitude, for focus and concentration, for meditation and discovery. We need to make ourselves a priority on that to-do list. We need to carve time out of our too busy days to stop multitasking and start weaving one row at a time.

We also need to carve out space, another element most of us have too little of in our crazy, busy lives. Though we somehow manage to make space for the 30-inch television screen, the computer, the stereo system, the exercise equipment, the kid's toys, the guest room, etc, etc., we seldom claim title to the space for our own creative impulses and expressions.

As I sit here writing, besides the beautiful views of flowers and trees and birds outside my many windows, I can also see other things inside the studio that please my eyes—carved owls, artwork, my frame drum, an embroidery one of my sons did in first grade, and seashells on the windowsills from travels with my family.

23

Within the space of this studio, my soul has space—to day-dream, ruminate, introspect, and create. Without this space, my soul and I feel confined.

Space is an important element in weaving. On the loom there is what looks like a huge comb of metal teeth called the reed. The job of the reed is to keep the threads evenly spaced across the loom and to beat the weft into the web. If there was no reed the edges of the weaving would become distorted and the fabric itself be uneven. There are different sizes of reeds that allow the weaver to put the threads either very close together (100 ends per inch) or much farther apart (4 ends per inch). The reason for spacing threads far apart is to create either a very airy, lacey fabric, or to allow for very thick or hairy yarns, such as mohair, to separate and allow the weft through. Threads are placed closer together for a more dense fabric or if the threads are very thin. The cotton used in sheets, for example, is so fine that it is placed 200 or more to an inch! Proper spacing in weaving allows for a more balanced, even, and integrated fabric.

Proper spacing, space for ourselves along with everyone and everything else, allows for more balanced, even, and integrated lives. We need space and just like the yarns, how much space is needed can vary from person to person.

I love watching decorating shows and many a show has inspired me to try something in my own home. One of the popular themes on these shows is how to make do with small spaces, from making the most of a small apartment, to creating space for a home office. One episode of Martha Stewart Living showed how to set up a sewing space in a closet—a small closet at that. She had her carpenter come in and design a drop-down table for the sewing machine, and all kinds of storage for fabric and threads and tools. When the owner of this sewing closet was done sewing for the day, she could move the sewing machine to the back of the closet space, drop down the table and close the door and no one would ever know she had a sewing space there. Great, right?

24

Yes—and no. While I know not everyone has enough rooms or enough space to create a sewing room or weaving studio, or a cozy nook to read and relax, or a meditation space to find that quiet place within us, still our objective should not be to see how small a space we can take up, but how big a space we can reasonably claim. Making our time and our creative play or relaxation or spiritual explorations a priority means claiming enough space for that activity including the creative chaos and mess that may come with it.

Some of the textile arts take very little room. Knitting is handy because as long as you have a bag big enough to carry the long needles, your pattern book, and a ball or two of yarn, you are good to go. Ditto crochet, embroidery, needlepoint, and some stages of quilting. Portability, after all, is what made needlework such a feminine art—we could take it anywhere we needed to in order to supervise and care for the children, the sick, and the elderly. But once you begin to sew, quilt, weave, paint, or practice yoga, then you need space. And you don't just need space for equipment; you need space to be messy, disorganized, and creatively chaotic! For creative expressions, you need a space where you don't have to clean up after every session of work. Carving out time for your own creative play is hard enough, but if part of that time has to include ten to fifteen minutes of set-up and another ten to fifteen of take-down and clean-up, then you are likely to feel stressed and frustrated and give up on your creative efforts. If you want a space for reading and relaxing, writing in your journal, or practicing yoga, then you need room for tables and shelves or floor mat and stereo. Here, too, it is helpful if you don't have to spend precious time setting up and taking down or putting away.

When I am in the middle of a big project such as getting ready for a craft show, or working on a new palette or design, my studio floor is covered with cones of brightly colored yarns I have pulled from the walls to see how they interact with each other. Thread ends from a finished weaving may hang from the loom or lay scattered about the floor. Magazines and books

25

may lay open on my worktable so I can get color and design ideas. And while I can only stand this chaos for so long, it only gets put away when I am ready to put it away—when the project is done or the design laid out. I do not have to clean up at the end of the work period or day in case someone might see the mess, just as my husband does not have to clean up his mess in his shop from his latest woodworking project.

Whether it's "a room of one's own" or a chair and a lamp, we need our personal space, other than the traditionally designated kitchen. We must first decide how much personal space we need and in how many places. For instance, the kitchen might be one place we play and express ourselves, but we might also want a comfortable place to put our feet up and relax or read or just daydream. We might want a space big enough for a sewing machine and a quilting frame, or just a corner of a room for a cupboard to store our yarns and books on knitting, along with a chair and a basket to hold our current project. We might need a drawer next to the bed to store our journal and special pens, or we might need an entire desk in a room with a door that closes where we can sit and compose the next Pulitzer.

Some of us may be perfectly happy with a small, cozy space. Some of us may want to have room to stretch. My husband and I live in an old farmhouse with plenty of rooms and square footage. Now that our three boys are grown and out of the house, people continue to ask me if I mind the empty house. Mind? No way! I love the sense of space I feel now. I am like that fuzzy mohair. I love lots of space inside and out. Those three active boys and their energy filled every room in the house while they were growing! Now, I can let my energy fill some of those spaces and I love it.

Once your space is claimed, don't just make it functional, make it beautiful—make it sacred. Here's why. If the space, no matter how small, is beautiful, it will lift your heart and your smile every time you enter it. If you make it sacred, blessing it with your hopes and prayers, then every time you enter it, you will in turn feel blessed and the work you do there will be blessed. And in the blessing, you will know the value of who you are and what you do. Your time there, however long or brief, will be spent in conscious awareness and you will have an oasis of renewal for your heart and mind and soul.

The tendency is for us to keep putting off creating space for ourselves until the kids are gone, or a bigger house is purchased, or we have retired. Don't wait! Create a space for yourself—as big as you can make it—only for yourself. Yes, you can have guests stay in it once in awhile, but be sure to reclaim it! Make it beautiful, make it sacred, and then, whatever you do there, the time you spend in it will be healing and nurturing.

THRUMS

  ❧ How much time a day do you set aside for yourself to relax, daydream, or work on something you love? If the answer is none, what prevents you and how can you change that?

  ❧ How much time per week do you give yourself to play, relax, get away, or get going on a project? Who do you need to ask for help so you can have that time? Who do you need to say no to?

  ❧ If you can't imagine what you would do with this gift of time, notice what things other women find time to do that makes you envious. Or ask yourself what activity gave you pleasure as a child. Would you like to do that now?

  ❧ How much space do you need to do an activity that brings you pleasure and moves you into a quiet place? Are you including room to be openly messy?

  ❧ How can you make your space however small or large, beautiful and sacred? Do you need to include a candle and some flowers in the space? Pictures of loved ones? Artwork to inspire? Do you have music?

❧ Now look at your to-do list and put your special activity at the top of the list and make time for it so at the end of the day you can cross that off the list with joy and a genuine sense of accomplishment! Make sure to include it on tomorrow's list—and no multitasking!

Lesson Four

STRUCTURE—
FINDING FREEDOM IN LIMITATIONS

"I think knowing what you can not do is more important
than knowing what you can do."
~ LUCILLE BALL

"I could never work with great spirit in any material unless I knew that the
amount of it was limited—I had to be hedged in by a boundary of either
space or material, in order to awaken the feeling of creative excitement."
~ KATHERINE BUTLER HATHAWAY

ARLY IN HER TUTELAGE, A WEAVER DISCOVERS THAT
she cannot weave a perfect circle into her fabric.
Because of the up and down, side-to-side nature of
weaving, creating a circle in a woven design requires a little
fudging. It is like trying to create a circle on graph paper by filling in the squares—you can get pretty close but the circle will
never be perfectly round, its edges always slightly bumpy. That
horizontal over vertical structure of the woven cloth is a direct
result of the horizontal and vertical structure of the loom.
Learning to work within those two inherent structures of
framework and fabric is the challenge for the weaver.

While this structure may appear limiting at first, without it
no weaving could be done. Any weaver will tell you that to try
to weave without the loom to provide tension to the warp, and
to keep the threads in a certain order and spaced in a certain

way, is to face a tangle of threads with no clear relation to each other and no way to open a path for the weft. The two structures, that of the loom and that of the woven fabric, create limitations of size, technique, length and width, but inherent within those structures are the pathways through chaos to freedom.

Maybe that is why I was drawn to the loom and weaving. Although I took classes in drawing, sewing, quilting, and machine embroidery, when it came time to use these techniques for my own artistic expression, I was overwhelmed by all the possibilities. Feelings of inadequacy and fear of failure hit me. The opportunities for "wrong" choices and "mistakes" seemed too great.

But limitations of the loom limited my fear by narrowing both the field of choices and the opportunities for doing it wrong. For instance, I can only weave the width of the loom. Any patterns are limited by the number of harnesses (the frames of heddles that lift the threads up and down) on the loom. I can only weave the length of the warp. And, because of the inherent nature of weaving, as mentioned earlier, a weaver is always creating within the grid of the horizontal and vertical threads. Curves are possible only within a grid pattern, however small or subtle. Limitation upon limitation! Choices made for me before I throw the first weft! How freeing!

At the time I was working on my MFA, I explored a weaving technique, double-weave pick-up, which allowed for a free development of pattern and image within the work. It is an ancient technique found most often in South America and Finland and allows the creation of pictorial designs. Though intimidated by the thought of doing a painting in watercolor or oils, by working on my loom with this two-layered weave of different colored threads, I was able to create symbolic and representational images with thread that would not occur to me in another media. Only with these boundaries of possibilities, could I weave—in a sense, paint—with freedom.

The structure did not tell me what images to make, nor

what colors to use. Those were my choices, my decisions. But my shapes could only be so round, and color effects and shading were limited once the warp colors were wound onto the loom.

Through the loom and that doubleweave technique, I learned that structure is not only a good thing; it is a necessary thing. Like the beams and castle (the upright supports) of the loom, the bones of our body keep us erect and organized for movement and action. Without our bones, we would be a floppy Raggedy Ann doll, lying immovable until someone or something came along and shifted us. Without structure—the beams and castle of the loom, the bones of our body, or the steel beams and wooden studs of our homes, one huff and puff of the wolf would certainly blow us, and everything else, down.

It is the paradox of human nature that we constantly strive to break free from limitations of structure while also finding comfort and refuge within them. From our first steps as a toddler to our first time as a teenager driving a car, we do not want limitations. We don't want anything or anyone to get in our way, to tell us no. And yet, in the best of circumstances, as we grow up, our families and communities provide structures and frameworks of routines, rules, expectations and limits based on beliefs and values that give us something to push against, to push through, to change or question, and thereby help define who we are and who we are yet to become.

Though I had my own small rebellions against structure in my youth—writing an underground newspaper for my high school (where my father was president of the school board) deploring teacher unions and tenure, and trying my first taste of alcohol and cigarettes in college—I gradually discovered the role and importance of structure first through my marriage, then through parenthood and finally through my weaving.

At our wedding, Bob and I took vows of commitment and faithfulness that are part of the structure of marriage. In doing so, we put aside the consideration of others as intimate emotional or sexual partners. We did this with a whole-hearted conviction that we truly loved each other and would work hard to make our marriage work. This freed me to give my energy to making friends with other men, and to working with them but not to being distracted by other possibilities. The friendships are clear and strong and so is my relationship with my husband.

When raising our three sons, my husband and I, believing in the importance of routine for children, established the structure of rules about bedtimes, curfew, and homework. This structure minimized for my husband and I recurring negotiations for later bedtimes, or when to come home, or the importance of homework. In fact, my husband and I discovered that our three sons actually craved and thrived on structure. Yes, they occasionally rebelled against and questioned rules and routines, but they also used them to protect themselves and to find direction and certainty in questionable situations.

For instance, if they felt uncomfortable going somewhere or doing something, they would ask us if they could go, wait for the "no" that was sure to come—or ask for it, if it didn't—then turn around and tell their friends that their parents wouldn't let them. We gladly played bad guys so our sons wouldn't lose face with their peers.

We also established parameters and expectations for them about sex, drugs, and alcohol. The personal, social, and legal ramifications, the limitations created by their abuse, were made clear to them. To that end, we always expected to know where they were, to have a phone number to be able to reach them (before the days of personal cell phones), and to know when they were expected to return. Did they whine and moan and groan against these rules? Yes. Did they probably bend and break them on occasion? Yes. Do we believe those limitations made a difference anyway? Absolutely.

Too few limitations mean too many choices for adolescents suffering from a burden of pressures and expectations from peers and society that can make choosing wisely for themselves difficult and frustrating. If nothing else, limitations encourage them to pause and think before pushing past them.

Establishing our core beliefs and values as partners and parents, then creating the structures of marriage and parenthood around our sons and ourselves gave us all something to push and even kick against, and, more often, shelter under.

What defines us as adults, of course, is when the structure in our lives comes from within rather than being imposed upon from without. When we start to shape our lives around our own tested beliefs and values such as responsibility to our parents or loyalty to friends, as well as move past limitations that are no longer valid, we are building the internal structure that will help us weave our life with integrity.

I discovered the need to move past old limitations and to test the structure of my identity as wife, mother and weaver when I first exhibited and sold at craft shows. Up to that time, I was a timid driver and seldom drove on heavily trafficked interstates more than 30 miles beyond home, at least not without my husband with me. Big city highways especially intimidated me with their fast-moving traffic that constantly changed lanes. But in my first year of exhibiting, most of the shows I chose were located in urban environments like Pittsburgh, Boston, Philadelphia, and Washington D.C. My husband could not go with me to these shows since our three sons were still under the age of sixteen, and someone needed to stay home and care for them. I had to drive myself—down unfamiliar roads, in and out of heavy traffic. Before each trip, I laid out my itinerary, making sure I had clear directions. Then, I put my fears in the back seat, and I drove from two-lane county routes to six-lane interstates. Soon I was driving into Philadelphia, Boston (an insane place to drive!), and even on the Beltway around Washington D.C. I quickly discovered that with each journey, my fears diminished.

Tony Robbins, personal empowerment coach, says that each of us has a circle of comfort within which we move and act with ease but that by pushing just beyond the limit of a fear in one area, we affect how we feel about other fears within that circle of comfort and thus enlarge the entire circle. I had done

33

just that—increased my comfort zone and removed some of my limitations.

Moving beyond limitations is a good thing in our efforts to grow into our true potential. Too often though, fear encourages us to stay within the limitations, sheltering under the old, reliable structures we have built for our lives.

Ironically, these structures can become prisons if they are deemed to be perfect and inviolable. Here lies the road to obsession, arrogance, and revolt. Structures are not meant to be prisons. They are created to serve people, not the other way around.

Imagine if the weavers of long ago decided that there was only one perfect structure for a loom—the weavers of the Southwest and South America where wood is scarce and lifestyles are more nomadic, would have had a hard time dragging my type of 60 inches wide floor loom, a European style, from summer pasture to winter encampment, not to mention even finding enough wood and other materials to build it in the first place. And the innovative Chinese would never have built room-sized looms with many harnesses that allowed for the weaving of complex fabrics suitable for strong silk threads.

It is the principle or purpose of the loom, its structure, to create tension on the warp thread that is primarily important and manifests itself in so many interesting variations from culture to culture, family to family, weaver to weaver. So while I am a big proponent of marriage, for example, it is the principle of the structure—a committed, loving relationship—that is important and can vary in infinitely wonderful ways depending on cultural, societal, and religious beliefs and values.

Over time and use, though, structures decay, become outmoded, even restricting. Then we need not only to push against them but to tear them, or some part of them, down.

My husband and I live in an 1840's Greek Revival farm house. When we went to remodel the kitchen, we discovered that part of the floor and the back wall had rotted from water damage. So, our contractor ripped out the floor and back wall, studs and all, and replaced them. The rotted part of the structure endangered the rest of the house with shifting weight, spreading rot, and a susceptibility to insects. The new studs and new wall meant a stronger, more durable structure. We would have been crazy to continue to live within the structure as it was until it decayed and fell down around us. We could have moved out, sold the house, and bought a new one. But we chose to repair it—we valued the structure that was our home.

Sometimes the structure is not decayed but just weakened. Like our home sometimes all the structure needs is repairing or tightening up.

As a weaver, I periodically tighten the wing nuts and screws on my loom as the constant' vibrations and stress of weaving shakes them loose. Then my weaving can lose its evenness or I can't beat the weft into the fabric as tightly as I want. Pushing against the structures in our lives shakes things loose too and gives us an opportunity to either reevaluate those structures— beliefs, values, and commitments—or to tighten up the few loose screws and wing nuts.

My husband and I love to travel long distances in the car because this gives us the quiet time away from work, phone, house projects, etc. to just focus on each other, to have long, lengthy, quiet conversations about family, friends, and our dreams. In those conversations we tighten the wing nuts and loose screws of our marriage, and when we return from our trip we are ready to begin once again living within and pushing against the structure of our commitment to each other.

Structure and its inherent limitations are an important part of life, and we need to be ready, and willing, to tighten them when they loosen, reevaluate them as they age, and tear them down when they decay or stop serving their purpose.

We need strong structures within which to weave our lives.

35

THRUMS

- What organizational structures such as family, church, school, or government have you found useful in your life? How have they been useful?

- What are the core beliefs and values by which you live your life? Are they still effective? How are they reflected in the structures—marriage, parenthood, career, religious affiliation—of your life?

- What personal structures keep your life running smoothly and minimize chaos? What ones need to be released, and what new ones need to be integrated into your life?

- Are you feeling restricted by a structure in your life as it is currently configured? Do you need to change it, adapt to it, push against it, or tear it down? If you tear it down, with what will you replace it?

- What activity or action lies just beyond your comfort zone, the structure of limitations? What can you do to move beyond it?

- Take a walk in the basement of your house or building. Look at how the foundation is constructed, how the beams cross and support each other like a weaving. Think of how strong they must be to support the weight of your home. How strong are the supporting structures of your life? Do any screws or wing nuts need to be tightened?

36

Lesson Five

INTENTION AND PERSPECTIVE— CREATING THE VISION

"Creativity comes from trust. Trust your instincts.
And never hope more than you work."
~ RITA MAE BROWN

"The core of creation is to summon an image
and the power to work with that image."
~ ANAIS NIN

REMEMBER HOW MANY OF OUR FAVORITE FAIRY-tales begin with a woman expressing her heart's deepest desire? Often that desire, as in Snow White, Sleeping Beauty, Thumbelina, and Rapunzel, is a woman longing to give birth to a child. The story does not really begin until the vision or intention is expressed. Then magic happens.

In order to wind a warp for the loom, I must first express or envision what I want to weave. The "story" of my weaving will not come to a happy ending if I wind a narrow warp of seven inches, put it on my loom, and then decide after the warp is threaded and tied on that I want to weave a shawl that is twenty-eight inches wide. I must then either unthread that warp, putting it aside, and wind on a new one that is the required width, or I can weave off the narrow warp first and then put on the wider warp for that shawl. Either option wastes time, effort, and perhaps even yarn. I will not be able to make up this loss later.

For our lives to unfold like the fairy tales of old, we must express the intention or vision for our lives—our heart's deepest desire.

In the last few decades, setting goals in both our personal and business lives has been popular and very helpful. But goals are only useful if they move us closer to our vision for our life. First, of course, we need to be able to identify what that vision or intention is.

In my mother's generation, a young woman grew up knowing that the vision for her life, like the heroines of those fairytales, generally revolved around creating a home for husband and children. For my mother, while husband and children were an important part of her vision or life dream, being an artist was equally important. So going to art school after high school was a goal that would move her closer to her vision. Unfortunately, because of family finances and the fact that her father lost money at the track on a regular basis, there was no money for art school.

My mother's maiden aunt offered to pay for tuition at a secretarial school. At that time, being a secretary was an acceptable career for women until marriage and children came along. So my mother went to secretarial school and then took a job with the CIA where she worked until she met my father, fulfilling at least part of her life vision of husband and children.

In spite of not attending art school, my mother found other ways to express her creative and artistic bent. She sewed clothes for herself and for my siblings and I that were stylish and lovely. At the holidays, she took great pleasure in fashioning unusual holiday decorations and gifts, and festooning the house with them. Her creativity even extended into entertaining family and friends with elaborate meals or theme parties such as the luau she created for a church group. Guests that night were greeted with paper leis and walked into a house filled with hula music and lit by blue and pink light bulbs. Dinner was eaten from low tables while sitting cross-legged on the floor. The meal included barbecued pork, pineapple, and even nonalcoholic drinks with little umbrellas.

Through it all, she never let go of her desire to study art. When my siblings and I were old enough to all be in school during the day, my mother purchased a set of oil paints and brushes, and a few small canvases. She taught herself to paint, and looking out our dining room window, painted her first landscape.

Then, many years later when I was a teenager in high school, she enrolled in college as an art education major. Graduating with a master's degree, she took a position as an art teacher in a local high school. While teaching, she painted in watercolors, hoping to show her work in a local gallery. Recognizing the strength of her vision, my dad had a family room/ studio added on to our home.

Sitting before the studio window that looked out over the valley, Mom stroked color onto paper, the subjects of her paintings often of her second creative passion—antiques. She had a vision, a clear intention of the direction she wanted her life to take, and though part of the dream was delayed for a time, she continued to weave her way towards it, even after she became ill with breast cancer, retiring from teaching to paint full time and struggle with her health. Months after she died, her work was exhibited, as planned, with the work of a well-known artist friend, who helped fulfill Mom's lifelong dream. Though she did not choose the time of her death, my mother died having fulfilled her vision, having lived with intention.

Mom's life is an example of how, no matter the size or scope of the vision, if that vision or intention is strong enough, if it is committed to with passion and discipline, that vision will gather momentum and continue to move forward in spite of all obstacles, even death.

While some of us are fortunate enough to know what our lives are about almost from the moment of birth, the rest of us can move from age to stage and still be asking what we were meant to do and be, what our life is about. While women today have many more options for careers and personal lives than women of my mother's generation, sometimes it is those numerous options that can make identifying the dream or intention so challenging and even painful. We are unclear about our direction either because nothing pulls at us strongly enough or because we have so many different directions that intrigue us. We feel like Dorothy at the crossroads of Oz, wondering which way to go and the only advice we are given is that "… that way is a very nice way. Of course, some people do go that way …"

Here is where working with sleep dreams and daydreams, and keeping a journal can be especially helpful. Dreams often bring messages of the heart's yearnings, and offer ways to move toward them. The journal, over time, mirrors back through daily events and encounters what at the moment may be only vague images of unexpressed urgings.

Several years before I became a professional weaver and writer, I had a dream that alerted me to the importance and vitality of my own heart's desires. In the dream, I am Egyptian royalty on my way to the temple to celebrate some ritual. My chair bearers bring me to the steps of the temple and as I am about to step out of the chair and ascend the steps, a man of the servant class steps out of the temple and unrolls a long strip of papyrus and reads it aloud. On it are scribed a list of demands from the people in the temple. I nod to one of the priests standing behind the man, intending for the priest to take the man into custody so I can speak with him later. Instead, the priest pulls a knife from his robes and stabs the man in the back. I am horrified at being misunderstood and for causing the death of the man.

After recording the dream and writing my thoughts about it in my journal, I finally understood its essential message—I was killing the very ideas and visions, those beings from the temple who were demanding my attention, that would lead me to my life vision as an artist and writer. I was killing them unintentionally, of course. The dream was very clear about that. But

I was still killing them. With the gift of that dream, I paid attention to where I let myself abdicate responsibility for my creativity, where I sabotaged and even killed my creative impulses and ideas. Where before, I let the daily demands of three young sons, and the never-ending need for cleaning and maintenance of our old farmhouse usurp my time, I now made my creativity a higher priority. I took it and myself more seriously.

And isn't that what happens to all of us along life's journey? We get caught up in the day-to-dayness of living, of moving through the moments of our lives without awareness. Before we know it, the vision, the intention for our life is soon buried and forgotten.

In addition to dreams and journals, taking a class in something we are interested in helps unearth those buried longings. Another strong clue to rediscovering a forgotten vision or passion, as Julia Cameron suggests in her book *The Artist's Way*, is to look at whom you are jealous of. If you find yourself turning the color of lime Jello because a friend just landed a great job with an ad agency, or your sister-in-law just published her first book, then that might be a sign that they are taking action on and achieving goals that you secretly cherish for yourself.

Sometimes, when we have lost touch with the intention for our life, we will follow what appear to be detours but in fact are our paths in disguise.

Although I always loved writing, I am also attracted to many forms of creativity as well as to spiritually oriented professions. Even when trying to choose a college major, I was uncertain about which path to follow. At first I majored in French, a language I first discovered when I was seven and had remained interested in, thinking to become an interpreter.

But, after the first year of struggling to keep up with suburban classmates who had had the advantages of language labs and trips to France and Canada for language immersion, I knew I, the rural school girl, didn't love the language enough to do the work required to close the gap. So then, what to study? I considered Art History, but realized there really was no question of a major for a girl who had been reading and writing stories since she was five. I declared my major in English/Creative Writing.

Unsurprisingly, there were few jobs for creative writers fresh out of college, especially one with no teaching certification. So my first full-time job was as a visual merchandiser —someone who dresses store mannequins and creates displays in the store windows—for Gimbels in Pittsburgh. I found the job interesting but thought it was just a stopgap measure until I could find my "real" job.

In the second year of marriage, my husband and I moved to the Washington DC area, so he could study for his master's degree at Georgetown. The job I found there was as a telephone information assistant in Subscriber Services with Blue Cross and Blue Shield. I was in that position for less than a year when I was promoted to secretary of the Assistant Manager of Subscriber Services. A year later, I was promoted to secretary for the Manager of Training. None of these jobs required the best of my writing skills, though I did volunteer to write articles for the in-house magazine.

While I worked as a secretary, I also studied a range of needlework techniques with a local fiber artist. I had learned to sew from my mother, and to knit, crochet, and do embroidery from my aunts and grandmother, but for the first time, while studying with that fiber artist, I learned to use yarn and needle in the same fashion as paint and brush. I loved it, and continued to study needlework, uncaring whether it led me closer to my life's vision of being an artist and writer.

I became pregnant and the following spring, Bob graduated. Our first son, Stephen, was born that summer and within a few months, Bob took a job as associate demographer for the state of New York, and that fall we moved to the Albany area. I was now a busy full-time mother, especially after the birth of our second child only fifteen months after the first!

Then I took a weaving course that launched a new career.

I was pleasantly surprised to discover, from the perspective of time, that everything I had done to that point assisted in my desire to become a professional weaver. The display work done for Gimbel's paid off in how to set up my booth for craft shows to ensure maximum drama and eye appeal for the customer. The customer service over the phone and the training of employees for Blue Cross and Blue Shield, gave me skills for dealing both with customers in the booth, and wholesale buyers over the phone. And my experience as a mother gave me the patience and insight to discover the rewards lurking behind the challenges. Though it might appear that in becoming a professional weaver I had veered away from my intention to become a published writer, in fact, the weaving pulled me inexorably in just that direction. This book is the proof!

Before sitting down to her loom to create an intricate landscape or other painterly design, a tapestry weaver must first define the vision or intention of her weaving by drawing her design onto paper the size of the finished piece. After adding color to the image, she then places the paper with the image, called a cartoon, underneath or behind the warp (most tapestry looms are vertical rather than horizontal), so she can follow the contours and shapes of the design while she weaves, as well as be reminded of the colors she wants to use in each area. In this way, the weaver is reminded of "the big picture" while weaving the small details of her unfolding vision.

In order to see how the multiple colored threads of my past fit into the weaving of my life, I need the perspective of time and distance. Like the tapestry weaver, I need to step back from my loom to see how colors are blending and to get a sense of the big picture. We know that when we bring a picture too close to our eyes, the outlines and colors blur, and the same can happen with our lives, making it difficult to get a sense of whether or not we are weaving the lives we imagined.

The stumbling block for so many of us is that we tend to look at our lives from the same point of view the tapestry weaver does. While she diligently weaves in the different areas of colors and shapes, she is looking at what will be the back of the tapestry where the ends of her yarns are left hanging from the surface. And, in many cases, the shapes of different colors have gaps or spaces between them that need to be sewn together for the tapestry to be finished. If all that the weaver looked at was that chaotic surface, she could easily believe that her design, her work, her vision was chaotic, even worthless. To get a true picture of her progress, she must either go to the back of the loom, if it is vertical, or slide a mirror underneath her weaving, if it is horizontal, so she can see the weaving as others will see it. To see what she is creating, she has to step back and see not just the whole weaving, but the whole weaving from a different angle as well.

As we move from event to event, from experience to experience, from one life stage to the next, we can feel that our life is nothing more than a messy weaving with ends of yarns hanging all over the place, making it hard to see any design or beauty in the piece. Our life viewed from that angle may feel like nothing more than one big chaotic mess.

To weave a life of color, texture and design requires a movement back and forth between intention and perspective. Designing a life with intention is useful and important—and our goals help move us toward that intention or vision. But, just as the tapestry weaver needs the cartoon to see the big picture, we must also take time to step back from the forward momentum of our lives to evaluate if we are getting where we want to go, and if not, to see where we need to make changes and adjustments in the weaving of our lives.

Sometimes, as in my case, time provides the necessary perspective. Also, here again is where our dreams and our journals are a valuable tool. Periodically reviewing events and dreams over a recent time period of weeks or months, even years, allows us to gain distance and perspective on our life and to see where patterns of choices and attitudes affect the weaving.

When these tools are not enough, we need to seek a different perspective from others—to see ourselves, our life weaving through the eyes and perceptions of another. Family and friends are a great resource for this, and some of them will be only too happy to share with you where they think your life is going wrong—so be careful to ask for perspective from someone who can offer it with love and compassion, as well as experience. The gift of insight from a close friend is precious, both in the asking and the giving.

If friends and family cannot offer you a clear perspective because of their own personal challenges or private agendas, then professionals such as coaches, ministers and therapists are a good alternative, as are support groups. In fact, in today's environment of constantly changing jobs and homes, these may be our only resource for stepping outside our narrow field of vision to see where our daily choices are leading us.

Seeking out those who can provide us with perspective is important, especially since they can help us see that the small detail of the weaving we may have focused on does not represent the entire weaving. Most of us tend to see ourselves as too small. After focusing on one area of our life weaving, such as our career, we can easily become convinced that that aspect represents our entire weaving, our entire life. Or we fail to see the level of influence or knowledge we have available to offer others. The perspective of others reminds us of how wide and how high our life is and can be.

Just as the driver of a car or the pilot in a plane is constantly making shifts and adjustments in direction to account for turns in the road or changes in the wind, getting perspective on our life, whether from our journal or our best friend, helps keep us aligned with our intention, our vision. And if we need to make a detour here or there, or an unscheduled stop, that does not mean that we can't get to where it is we want our lives to go.

We just need to have a vision or intention that is truly of the heart—compelling enough to draw us forward and to demand a commitment from us to stay the course to our journey's end.

THRUMS

- Do you have an intention or vision for your life not necessarily related to a career? If not, write down the request to have a dream that reveals your strongest desire or vision for your life. Put it under your pillow and go to sleep repeating the request in your mind. Then record any dreams in the morning, looking at them for clues. Don't be discouraged if you don't get something right away. Give the process and yourself time.

- If dreams don't seem to help, go through magazines and ads tearing out those images that tug at you. Use them to create a collage on paper or mat board. As in a dream, are there clues there to the vision that is calling you?

- Are you keeping a journal to help give you perspective? If long writing is not your thing, consider making daily lists. These could include lists of accomplishments, lists of concerns and fears, lists of people you have helped or been helped by. See any patterns?

- Who are two people, professional or otherwise, who you could ask for perspective on your life now?

Lesson Six

THE WARP—
WORKING WITH WHO WE ARE

"If we do not know our own history, we are doomed to live it as though it were our private fate."
~ HANNAH ARENDT

"Sometimes a person has to go back, really back—to have a sense, an understanding of all that's gone to make them—before they can go forward."
~ PAULE MARSHALL

AS A WEAVER, I MUST HAVE THREADS AND YARNS for both warp and weft with which to weave my fabric. Luckily for me some prehistoric woman more than twenty thousand years ago, needed thread or yarn as well before she could move from simple garments of skin and fur to more versatile garments of woven fabric.

I can imagine it must have been some wise woman pulling a comb of bone through her own snarled hair or that of her child, who first recognized how hair or fiber might be spun together to create string, thread, or even rope. From those first threads, women knotted, sewed, and then wove.

Older than weaving, spinning is an equally active archetype in the human imagination and language. The phrase "spinning a tale" probably evolved from the act of women sitting together spinning the wool or flax while at the same time spinning out stories to entertain themselves and the children they watched. Hence the recurring themes of spinning, weaving, and other needle arts in myths and fairytales such as Sleeping Beauty, who pricks her finger on a spindle, and Rumpelstiltskin, who spins all that straw into gold for a princess so she can win the hand of the king.

A weaver needs threads—thick or thin, smooth or fuzzy, delicate or strong—whether from the woolly fibers of the coats of sheep, the short fibers of the cotton boll, or from the long, shiny fibers created by the silk worm, who industriously chews thousands of mulberry leaves and then spins from itself the long, strong threads of silk. The amount of twist in the spun yarn of every natural fiber—wool, silk, linen, and cotton—as well as whether or not the fibers are parallel, can produce everything from the finest, smoothest silk, to nubbly cottons, to fuzzy mohair.

If you have ever been to a yarn shop, you have seen before you an array of choices, not only in color and fiber, but in texture and thickness as well, that is the equal of any artist's paint palette. One of my yarn suppliers has over 60 colors of one type of cotton alone. The number of possibilities for combinations of these yarns is endless!

Even working with the same yarn, any group of weavers can turn out very different fabrics depending on the patterns, colors, and combinations they use. I, for instance, work with rayon chenille, the softly fuzzy fiber that, when woven, feels like velvet. With its popularity among customers, numerous weavers over the last ten years have chosen to weave in chenille to create beautiful jackets, coats, sweaters, shawls and scarves for women. Yet each weaver's work is different from the other's. Sometimes the color choices make the difference; sometimes it is the choice of pattern or garment design. Whatever the reason, just like the gene combinations that created each of us, there is opportunity for unending variety and uniqueness.

The first threads or yarns I work with when beginning a new throw or jacket are the warp threads, the vertical threads in a woven fabric. Whatever I choose for the warp, it must be a relatively strong thread because it will have to withstand the tension of being stretched from the back beam of the loom to the front beam, as well as the friction of the reed as it moves forward and backward in the warp, beating each weft into place. Those strong warp threads are the foundational threads of the fabric—what the fabric is built on.

The warp threads of our lives are made up of our genetic heritage, our parents and siblings, our extended family, our homes and schools, and other early influences. Whether smooth or rough, dark or light, and strong or weak, these foundational threads are what we build our life on and contribute significantly to the unique person each of us is and will be.

These foundational threads, once wound on the loom, cannot be removed or changed until the fabric is woven off—not without seriously weakening or marring the fabric. They are the threads in our lives that appear early on, starting before birth and wind on through our growth as children into adolescence and even sometimes into early adulthood. These are usually the elements in our life that we feel were given to us, that we had little or no control over or did not consciously choose.

For example, few of us get to choose our parents. We do not get to interview them about their qualifications and goals for the job, ask them about their training, or years of experience. So, some of us luck out and have bright, colorful threads of childhood provided by parents who not only passed on healthy, intelligent genes to us, but also spent much of their love, time, energy and income to raise us. They generally helped us to see the world as a good place and life in it to be a good thing. If we were even luckier we had siblings we liked and extended family and friends who created a circle of protection and love around us.

Unfortunately, for many others, for whatever reason, childhood meant a constant struggle to survive amidst parenting that was sabotaged by lack of time, money, education, back-

49

ground, and resources. Maybe only one parent was present who struggled to do the best he or she could. Maybe there were two parents but other priorities got in the way of good parenting, whether because of too much money or not enough, too much work or not enough, or even because they were too young and not ready to be parents. Even if their intentions were the best, there are parents whose valiant attempts were undermined by poverty that led to less than an ideal community or family environment for raising kids and may have even led to violence, abuse, and addiction. We might wish to hide these darker threads, or even cut them away, but we can't. They remain part of our warp.

Our genetic heritage is another part of our life weaving that we did not choose, but came to us from our parents, and their parents before them and beyond, giving us predilection for diseases like heart disease, stroke, and cancer hidden in the bodies we were born with. Some of us are tall and dark. Others of us are short and fair-skinned. Some of us have blonde hair, some red, some brunette, some black. Some of us have straight-as-a-stick hair, while others of us have hair so curly it would be twice the length should we ever be able to straighten it out.

As women, most of us can relate a tale of growing up when at one point in our lives (usually our teens), we decided we didn't like some or all aspects of our physical appearance. For me, this hit when I was thirteen and had been menstruating for a short time. The first thing my newly activated hormones did was blow up my hips—not my breasts, mind you. My hips. And as if to add insult to injury, I had inherited the short-waistedness of my father along with the hippiness of my mother's side of the family, resulting in, as the style books describe it, the classical pear shape.

Well, it may be classical but it felt more like a curse when, that year, my mother took me shopping for an Easter dress. Everything I tried on that day as we traveled from department store to department store was either too big in the shoulders and bust or too small in the hips—my first experience of the dressing room blues. My poor mother, tired but patient, finally found a navy blue cotton Empire-waist dress with a white tucked bib. Navy blue for Easter! I was devastated as only a young teen can be. Where were the frills (I am sorry, tucking doesn't count), where were the laces and ribbons and colorful flowers? Glumly, I assented to purchasing that navy blue dress—and hated clothes shopping thereafter for decades.

Some of us have serious physical challenges that must be lived with everyday and that create limits on what we can do. My own small challenge was the asthma I had as a teenager that limited my ability and interest in physically demanding activities like swimming. Since the water often seems to weigh heavily on my chest and I did not grow up near water, I have a fear of deep water, even after taking two semesters of swimming lessons in college to overcome it. Fear has limited my ability to enjoy the ocean though I am determined to move past that some day.

Our environment and our education also make up the warp of our lives, especially because they often reflect the financial well-being of our family unit. Did we graduate from high school, go onto college, or was success defined as getting to school each day without violence? Did our parents value an education or was school just something to get through until the state said we were old enough to get a job? Did an unexpected pregnancy throw an unplanned thread into our warp?

The challenge for all of us is to accept these threads of our warp and work with them to create beauty. Wishing it wasn't so, ranting about the unfairness of our early lives, blaming our parents for a less than ideal childhood, can keep us from weaving a satisfying life. We can stare at the dark threads of our warp forever and fail to weave new beauty into our lives. Or we can see how the shadows of our past throw the present and the future into greater light.

As long as we bemoan the past we remain victim to it. We all know people both famous (Oprah comes to mind) and not famous, who had childhoods that were challenging and painful enough to make most of want to crawl in a hole and never come out. From the testing of those dark threads, they took strength to weave a future of beauty and hope that serves as models for the rest of us. Knowing that others have suffered and yet continue to weave rich lives, how can we do less?

My mother's older sister tells stories of growing up with her mother and father. Her father often became verbally and occasionally physically abusive after a bad day at the racetrack or work. One evening, when my mother was in high school and the prom was coming up, her father arrived home at the dinner table ready to take out his frustrations of the day on anyone. This time is was my mother. He challenged her with lying about something that had happened at school. When my mother denied the lie, a disagreement escalated into a screaming match. The loser was my mother. Her father ordered her to her room and forbid her attendance at her prom. My aunt, determined to not let her sister suffer for their father's sins, helped my mother sneak out of the house on her prom night for an evening of dancing and forgetfulness.

Hearing that story years after my mother's death, I marveled at the patient understanding my mother brought to her parenting in spite of the experiences with her father. Did that mean she didn't have her periods of yelling? Oh, no! But she worked hard to move past her anger into a place of understanding and forgiveness with us. And she never excused her own yelling or anger with tales of her father. I never heard the prom night story from her.

We can become so fixated on the dark threads that we fail to see the contrast, texture, and character that these threads add to the design of our life fabrics. If we spend our time bemoaning and blaming the past, we fail to see the opportunities to weave a better life from it.

But if we can look at the warp of our lives with an objective and forgiving eye, then we move forward to weave in the necessary wefts, the choices and actions, that will effectively integrate those dark threads without which our life weaving would be less beautiful, less strong, less whole.

Before I weave the weft into the warp, the colors of the

warp can look too bright or too dark, or have too much contrast or not enough. If I were to judge the fabric based on the warp alone, I might find it harsh or garish—less than beautiful.

In fact, it is only when I weave in the weft threads that an integrating, softening effect occurs. It is only after the fabric is off the loom and finished, that the totality of the weaving and the blending of the colors can be seen and appreciated.

Whether we wish to cover over those dark warp threads—and we can—or to weave in colors that will blend with and soften them, or even use those dark threads to make the bright threads brighter, the warp remains. It is who we are.

Take the gifts of those threads and use them to make you stronger, brighter, and more beautiful. Use them to weave a life of meaning from lessons learned from the past. Honor the bright threads and their memories; grieve the dark ones and then move on.

The weaving of your life is waiting. Make a choice to live in the present and move into the future. Pick up the thread of your life, and as you weave over and under each warp, acknowledge its role and its gift.

53

THRUMS

- ❧ Who are the people in your past that helped wind bright warps into your life weaving? What gifts did they give you?

- ❧ Who are the people in your past that wound in the dark or ugly threads? What did you learn from them? How has it shaped your life's weaving?

- ❧ If you had to choose colors to represent each member of your family what would they be? Can you find yarns or ribbons of those colors?

☙ Can you arrange those ribbons in a pleasing relationship to each other?

☙ What color can you put with those ribbons that would
make them more attractive to your eye? What experience or person does it represent?

Lesson Seven

THE WEFT—
CHOOSING TO CREATE BEAUTY

"It's when we are given choice that we sit with the gods
and design ourselves."
~ DOROTHY GILMAN

"... for beauty is simply Reality seen with the eyes of love."
~ EVELYN UNDERHILL

WHILE THE WARP THREADS ARE FOUNDA-tional, giving strength and durability to the weaving and once wound onto the loom cannot be changed, the weft threads are woven in with choice, sometimes spontaneously, and sometimes with great thought and intention, and can enhance the beauty and uniqueness of the weaving.

Even though each of us can choose from a similar selection of threads—education, career, family, and friends—every woman's weaving is unique. The color and texture of those threads, which ones she chooses and how she weaves them in, if at all, are what makes each woman's life different from the next.

Some threads, like education and marriage, can be woven in at any time, and for some of us, more than once! And yet others, like motherhood, once passed over, disappear from our selection of threads and may not be picked up later.

55

While some of those threads provide the highlight and sparkle to the life tapestry, others provide rich but subtle undertones. Not every thread, such as marriage or motherhood, is right for every woman, and will be like the woolen underwear of days gone by, serviceable perhaps, but an itchy fit at best.

These weft threads that we weave into our lives day after day, year after year are the fun part and the hard part at the same time. The fun part is that we get to choose. The hard part is that we get to choose. Depending on how much risk and fear is involved, making choices requires awareness and courage. And we can only make those choices one at a time, moment by moment.

I learned the challenge of this moment-by-moment, thread-by-thread process years ago when I was creating double-weave wall-hangings. Doubleweave is an ancient technique for creating pattern and design by weaving two interlaced layers of fabric at the same time. Each row of weft that the viewer sees actually represents two shots of weft—one in the visible top layer, and one in the hidden bottom layer. One layer created the background or negative space, while the other layer created the design or positive space. I had to be aware of how both were evolving at the same time.

The process required several steps for each shot or throw of weft. Each time I picked up the threads of the bottom layer with a knitting needle to be woven or interlaced into the top layer I had to make choices. Were the positive shapes going to get bigger or smaller? Sharply angled or softly rounded? Row by row I made choice after choice, weaving symbolic and representational images. It was a Zen-like practice in which I had to stay present with the weaving and the process. I could not rush it. It took an hour of uninterrupted work and concentration to weave one inch!

And so I became aware of the importance of choice and decision. Make the wrong choice and I could spoil the image. Then I would have to spend at least as much time correcting it.

Too, each choice I made had to take into account the warp

I was weaving over and under with each weft. The weft did not create shape or color by itself. In fact, the color effect was rather like a pointillist's painting—that is, where two threads crossed, two points of color crossed as well, the color of the weft and the color of the warp. One color either intensified the other, neutralized the other, or created a third color.

Depending upon how you feel about your foundational warp threads, you can use your daily life choices in the same way: to intensify, neutralize, or create a new color with them. For instance, I was lucky enough to have a father who was committed to family and community. He and my mother celebrated their thirty-second wedding anniversary several months before she died of breast cancer. My father served on our school system's board for at least the entire time I was in school and, in fact, handed me, his oldest child, my diploma.

I was happy to intensify the color of that warp thread with the choice of my husband. Though only a sophomore in college when I met him, I soon saw that same commitment to family and community in his connection with his siblings, and in his service to the community, as he organized and directed a fraternity fundraiser for a children's hospital. Years later, as president of our local school board, he handed his oldest child, our son, Stephen, his high school diploma as well. And we recently celebrated our thirty-second wedding anniversary.

57

For those whose foundational warp threads are not so fortunate or happy, making different choices about life partners, careers, where to live, how to parent, can serve to neutralize or create a new color from those life experiences while adding depth and beauty to the weaving.

I know a woman writer and editor who experienced the trauma and nightmare of violence and abuse as a young girl. Using fairytales as a way out of her situation in her imagination, she kept body and soul together until she was old enough to escape the situation. As an adult, she now weaves the colors of those fairytales, their language, history and understanding, into her life weaving as author and editor. These bright threads cross the darker ones of her past and thereby create a new color in the weaving and a new expression of self. The added blessing of this, of course, is that her stories and her work show other women with similar childhood experiences how to weave brighter colors of understanding and expression into their own life weavings.

Deciding to marry, whether or not to have children, whether or not to accept that job promotion, where to live, are important decisions that are like thick chenilles or fuzzy mohairs in our life weaving—they take up a lot of space in the warp and their effect on the whole weaving is obvious. We usually understand the importance of giving care and consideration to these life choices. The weft we weave in can cover the dark warp underneath. While we remain aware of the presence of those dark threads and how they contribute to the fabric of who we are, good parenting of our children can help subvert the poor parenting of our own mothers and fathers.

Although the big choices or decisions of our lives may take up considerable space in our life's weaving, the day-to-day choices and the mindful awareness we bring to them have an equally significant impact.

For me, raising three sons was a challenge similar to weaving those doubleweave pieces. I had to stay aware from moment to moment about the choices and decisions I made as a mother. From the start, there were, of course, the big choices like having natural childbirth, nursing instead of bottle-feeding, and choosing to sing the boys to sleep versus letting them cry it out; big decisions because at that time all the childraising techniques my mother's generation had learned from Dr. Spock were being questioned by my generation of new mothers.

While those choices my husband and I made were important for the physical and mental well-being of our sons, our smaller, day-to-day actions insured our sons' emotional and spiritual well-being.

When the two older boys were toddlers, once a week I bundled them up for a trip to the library for story hour—a precious time for us all, as they were kept occupied and amused while I had time to find a new supply of books for my own entertainment and mental stimulation, as well as theirs. One day, I was running typically late, and as I struggled to get Christopher dressed, he fought and twisted from me, insisting to me, "I do it myself!" Since he was only two at the time, I am sure I could have sat on him and pulled his clothes on but as I saw the frustration in his little face and felt it echoed in mine, I sat back and took a deep breath. Who was I hurrying to story hour for— them or me? What was really important here?

Though I knew he would need help, I handed his shirt to him. I had to sit on my hands and bite my tongue while he pulled it over his head, then twisted and struggled to get his arms in the sleeves while time ticked on. Finally, red-faced, he asked me to help. And I did—help—holding out a shirt hem and pulling out a sleeve so he could push his arms through. Then with a sigh of satisfaction from both of us, we and his brother headed for the car, a little late, but a lot more at peace with each other.

In that small moment of choosing, we both learned something. Christopher learned that I was willing to let him try which also gave him permission to ask for help when he needed it. I learned that by staying in the moment and being lovingly patient, I could truly see my child and his needs, not just in that situation but in future ones as well, for there were many more episodes of Christopher wanting to do it himself! And, by acting from a place of clarity, I not only wove a weft of beautiful mothering into my life weaving that morning and in other times to come, I added a warp of love and beauty to his.

Here is one of the challenges of weaving those weft threads into our life. So often the wefts we choose for our lives not only affect our weaving but may also affect the life weaving of others, sometimes many others, because, as John Donne tells us, no man—or woman—is an island. With the freedom of choice comes the responsibility as well, and thus weaving our lives is best done with awareness and courage.

Awareness is best achieved by being present in the moment. It is hard to make a choice or decision if we are caught up in regret or longing for the past, or worry about the future. The dreaded Whatifs pop up. What if I do this and then ...? What if I don't do this and then ...? What if so-and-so doesn't like my choice or worse, won't like me once I have made the choice? What if he/she wants to leave me because of this choice? On and on and on ... The dreaded Whatifs make us uncertain and fearful.

Making choices means listening to our fears, judging whether they are false or valid, trusting our instincts and then taking action, taking risks in the midst of those Whatifs. Making choices requires courage.

Remember when the Cowardly Lion in the *Wizard of Oz* asks his friends, "What have they got that I ain't got?" and his friends, including Dorothy, all chorus back at him, "Courage!" He responds to their truthfulness with his own, "You can say that again!"

Like the Cowardly Lion, how many times a day does fear grab hold of us, making us want to either freeze in place or turn tail and run for the nearest hiding place? Once a day? Twice a day? Or every hour on the hour? Besides the outer fears of violence and catastrophe the news brings us everyday, are our own inner monsters—fear of loneliness, separation, isolation, and the one that taunts us most often when making choices—fear of failure, of not doing it right or not being good enough.

The need to make too many choices is what so often immobilizes us as women. The whispered question runs unbidden through our minds: "What if I make the wrong choice?" That fear can keep us from ever beginning anything—a relationship, a new job, a pregnancy, a weaving.

In the film *Indiana Jones and The Last Crusade*, Indiana Jones has battled his way to the last stage of his quest for the Holy Grail, the mythical cup of healing and eternal life. Following his father's instructions written in a journal, Indiana knows there is supposed to be a bridge from one section of the cave to another where the Grail is kept. The problem is, it appears as if there is no bridge, only a chasm so deep it seems to have no bottom. But his father, who lies dying behind him has told him to trust, to believe. Indiana wants to believe that bridge is there, yet as the camera shows a close-up of his face as he stares across the chasm, you can just imagine the Whatifs in his mind whispering of death and doom should he step into the unknown. After throwing some dust before him and getting some sense of where the bridge is, Indiana, like the archetypal Fool, steps into seeming nothingness, to find himself supported by the unseen bridge.

This scene is about courage, about the willingness to take a risk, a big risk, in the face of daunting dangers and challenges, and about having faith in our own inner knowing, trusting our instincts and intuition. Indiana trusts his father and his own experience and intuition. To not risk, to not step off the path would mean going nowhere, to stay frozen, or worse—to go backwards. And as every woman in labor can tell you, sometimes going backwards or stopping are not options!

Sometimes it is a good idea not to think too long about the risks but, as Indiana does, to move forward in spite of them, for the more energy we give to our fears by thinking about them, the larger and more intimidating they become.

When my boys were young, one of their favorite books I read to them was *There's a Nightmare in My Closet* by author and illustrator, Mercer Mayer. The picture book is about a boy who tells the tale of the monster in his closet. He always closes the door before climbing into to bed to sleep with his toy cannon and popgun at the ready. "One night," the boy tells us, "I decided to get rid of my Nightmare once and for all." So he turns off the light and waits in the dark until he can hear the Nightmare creeping toward him. He turns on the light, and catches the Nightmare sitting at the foot of his bed. After threatening to shoot the Nightmare with his popgun, and then doing it, the Nightmare cries. When he won't stop crying the boy takes him by the hand and tucks him into bed, only to have the Nightmare gesture for the boy to close the closet door. Then they both drift off to sleep with the little boy acknowledging that there might be another nightmare in the closet but that his bed isn't big enough for three.

I love this story because, of course, each of us is that little boy (or girl) wanting nothing more than to hide beneath the covers until the Nightmare (our fears) have gone away. Eventually, though, hiding is not satisfying anymore because our fear keeps niggling away at us. We have to take action and confront the fear. Confront it and discover that it is just as much afraid of us as we are of it. Only by confronting and facing our fears do they lose their ability to threaten and immobilize us.

For most women, unless we are doctors, policewomen, or soldiers, giving birth is the only time when we enter a battle between life and death. Here, the life of mother and child can often hang in the balance. More often, the call to courage for women is about quietly facing the every day personal challenges of expression, change, and loss, or the workplace challenges of defining roles, responsibilities, and behaviors, or the relationship challenges of vulnerability, trust, and forgiveness.

Each of these challenges holds an opportunity to strengthen our courage muscles and thereby weave in choices of beauty and integrity by confronting our fears and stepping into the unknown. If we can stay in the moment, be aware and awake, and follow the call of our hearts, trust our intuition, then we become a little stronger, we move beyond unnecessary limitations. We move closer to being who we truly are.

When the Cowardly Lion finally stands before the Wizard awaiting his reward of courage, he has already made the long journey up the Yellow Brick Road, combating his fears by facing the Wicked Witch of the West, using his own strengths while supported by the help of his friends. So, when the Wizard gives him his reward—it is not the courage he thought he didn't have but an acknowledgement of the courage he already possessed. We need to do the same for each other and ourselves, acknowledging both the courage already expressed and the continued courage in facing the myriad of choices we are required to make each day.

It may take years before the beauty and wisdom of those choices appears in our weavings. Like the finest cotton or silk threads, which can take anywhere from 20 to 200 shots of weft to weave an inch of warp, it takes many of the threads of our daily choices to fill a space in our life weaving. It may take a week, a month, a year, or a lifetime to discern the effect those small choices and decisions has on our lives, and for us to have enough of a perspective to see if they added beauty and strength to the weaving, or marred or weakened it in some way.

The tools mentioned at the beginning of the book such as keeping a journal and keeping track of our dreams, and other tools like exercise and meditation can help us maintain mindfulness about the threads we choose to weave into our life. And each choice we make can teach us something about making the next one.

Being creative, being a woman, being human, means braving up to face the challenges that rise each day with the sun. Making choices with courage helps us weave a strong and integrated fabric. Making choices with courage and awareness means we create beauty not only in our life weavings but in others' as well.

THRUMS

  ❧ What are the important threads you have chosen to weave into your life?

  ❧ What are the threads you wish to weave in?

  ❧ What fear, or Nightmare, have you failed to acknowledge by keeping it hidden in a closet that keeps you from weaving a particular thread into your life? Is it time for you to open the door on it, either on your own or with the help of friends or a professional?

❧ During the day, watch how many times the Whatifs gang up on you. What are they saying? Write it down. Then either burn the paper, stick it in the freezer, or bury it.

❧ The next time you find yourself unable to make a choice because of fear or uncertainty, OR you are making a choice automatically without thought, slow yourself down, take several deep breaths, and listen for that inner voice of guidance and wisdom. What is it trying to tell you?

❧ What action have you taken recently, no matter how big or small, that required you to face a fear? Did you give yourself credit for it? If not, do so now. Write yourself a brief note of congratulations and hang it where you can see it for a week or two OR go buy a picture or figure of the Cowardly Lion to remind you how he continued to move forward, up that Yellow Brick Road, with the courage he already possessed and in spite of his fears.

Lesson Eight

RIGID ATTITUDES—
LOOK GOOD OR FEEL GOOD

"'What I believe' is a process rather than a finality.
Finalities are for gods and governments, not for the human intellect."
~ EMMA GOLDMAN

"In this unbelievable universe in which we live, there are no absolutes.
Even parallel lines, reaching into infinity, meet somewhere yonder."
~ PEARL S. BUCK

SEVERAL YEARS AGO, I WROTE A PROFILE FOR A PRO-
fessional crafts magazine of another weaver who, like
me, also weaves luxurious rayon chenille throws. As
we talked about her weaving history, I was surprised to discover that one of her very first jobs after college involved
weaving carbon for the parts and bodies of stealth jets!
Astonished, all I could think of was how rigid and unpleasant
it would be to wear something like that, and how odd it must
be to work with it.

Most of us, when we think about woven fabric think about
cotton sheets, Oriental rugs, or perhaps even silky scarves. Few
of us think about anything woven with rigid materials since
most of the woven fabric in our lives we either wear or use to
soften our environment. After all, how many of us want to
drape ourselves in screening?

Why then do we choose to weave the threads of rigid attitudes, inflexible beliefs, and unrelenting righteousness into our lives?

Remember the importance of those strong warp threads? They need to be strong because they are under some tension in order to create an open shed for the weft. If you put a weft into the weaving that is rigid and inflexible, and the warp is too tight for it, threads will inevitably break. Because the warp threads have to do all the bending and need more space to do it, rigid wefts laid in next to one another tend to separate from each other. It is as if those rigid threads don't really want to become part of the fabric.

Obviously, rigid wefts are not friendly to other wefts or to the weaving as a whole. And, if it is a fairly large rigid thread (think big attitude), in addition to jeopardizing the warp threads with more stress and tension, it only serves to draw attention to itself.

A "my way or the highway" kind of rigid thread forces the rest of the weaving to form, conform around it. That stiffness and incapacity to be flexible does violence to the rest of the weaving. That kind of attitude does violence to the fabric of self, community, and society as well.

The attractive lure of rigid attitudes is that they seem to make life simpler. They appear to provide strength and structure to our life weaving. Once I have established what is right (and therefore, by default, what is wrong), then everything else just naturally hangs from that. I don't have to think anymore. If I am always right, if my political party is always right, if my faith is always right then the inevitable conclusion is—you and everything you believe in, if different from me, is stupid, wrong or even sinful! And though the clarity and simplicity of that attitude may make me feel better, did you notice how you wanted to take several metaphorical if not literal steps away from me—just as the more flexible threads separate and move away from the rigid ones in a weaving?

The problem is, life is seldom that simple or clear. Most of the time we don't want to have to deal with the muddy issues of life. We don't want to wait for the silt stirred up by the churning of the waters to settle so we can see what is before us. We want immediate answers, immediate reassurance that all is right with our world so we can move on with our lives and our goals—regardless of someone else's goals, or life, or world. If we can safely decide beforehand how things ought to be at any given moment, then we don't have to stay in the pain and discomfort of the moment—we can daydream about the future or wax nostalgic about the past. A black and white world is so much easier to deal with—and saves time.

Wait a minute, you might protest, didn't I say structures did that for us? Yes, and no. Structures establish boundaries and limitations that keep us from having to remake decisions—yes. But, and this is a big but, I also said that structures are there to serve people, not the other way around. And here is the big difference between structures and rigid attitudes. Structures serve people who agree to exist or work or worship within that structure. As adults we choose our structures. Rigid attitudes try to force a certain structure on others. Force is the key word here. The result of force is usually a stronger opposing force which creates an escalation of force, resulting in mental, emotional, spiritual or physical violence. Most wars are the result of rigid attitudes that attempt to force a set of beliefs, values, or ideals on others.

Remember that woven carbon mentioned at the beginning of this chapter? As a shawl, carbon fabric would fail miserably but it worked well to hide and protect that plane. That is what our rigid attitudes try to do for us—hide and protect us from all the things we fear: fear of not being loved or accepted, fear of disease and death, fear of humiliation and powerlessness, fear of poverty and violence. Our solution is to turn to institutions, leaders, and religions that we believe can provide us with guidance and direction and lift the burden of fear from us—and the burden of mindful choices.

Problems arise when we abdicate our minds and hearts to

structures outside of us. It can certainly take the pressure off of
us in regard to making daily choices, but in that direction and
easing of responsibility, comes a denial of our innate spiritual
divinity. After all, the ability to make choices for ourselves is an
important part of making us human and, in many spiritual and
religious understandings, key to our own spark of divinity. If
we abdicate to the seemingly select—ministers, priests, gurus,
and even worse, political leaders—our ability and responsibility to make choices, to act with awareness, we makes idols of
them, the very thing those Old Testament prophets railed
against. Abdication denies us our humanity—and can cause us
to deny others their humanity as well. Hate crimes, torture, violence in all its dehumanizing variety is the result of denying our
ability and responsibility to choose—and of denying choice to
others. In our desire to simplify our lives we can make ourselves
a lot lower than the angels.

Does this mean all religions, governments, principles, are
bad? No, it means we must continue to bend in our hearts and
minds and souls; to be willing to continually question what we
believe to be true, to take the risk of being wrong while being
compassionate, to take the risk of being hurt while being loving,
to be willing to integrate ourselves into the fabric of family, community and the world by staying aware and flexible.

When I first learned to weave at that class at the community center, of the five or so students in the class, most of them
chose to weave in colors of brown, cream and black. For them,
this eliminated worry about getting the colors "right." Each
time they changed weft, they didn't have to wrestle with new
choices about colors and how they worked together. Our attitudes and perspectives are often the result of this same kind of
mindset—it is so much easier to deal with a duality, the black
and white of right and wrong, than it is to see the beauty in a
world woven of many threads dyed in rainbow colors of time,
need, culture, and circumstances.

Although the weavings of those students were nice enough,
and exhibited the different types of weaving techniques, they

lacked energy, vitality, even beauty. Living or working in an environment of black and white, whether on the walls or in the rules can make life seem simple but can also drain energy, and even kill spontaneity, creativity, and passion. So even though we may think that our rigid attitudes will make us look good and gain us respect, our concern about appearances may actually undermine that goal, leaving us stranded from the web of community we were working so hard to be part of or finding ourselves surrounded only by other similar rigid attitudes. Then we may wonder why our lives seem so lackluster and without vitality and passion.

Staying flexible does not mean we don't have principles, beliefs, and values to live by—it just means that they should serve Life and Love, not constrain it. Like a tree sapling, a fabric is stronger and more beautiful when the threads are flexible.

This lesson from the loom was repeatedly confirmed, of course, while raising our three sons. My middle son, the philosopher, pushed and tested and debated with his father and me about every dictum we laid out. When he was in his teens, my beliefs and attitudes were held up for examination on a regular basis. He challenged my husband and I to re-evaluate almost everything. This re-evaluation often led to shouting matches but it forced me to think about whether the beliefs I had had since childhood were still valid, whether the assumptions I made were based on personal observation or on somebody else's, and whether once serviceable structures from childhood had turned into rigid attitudes. It is natural for us as children to adopt the beliefs and values of our parents—and thereby become equally rigid—but can we or our children rightly claim adulthood until we have reevaluated those beliefs and values based on new perspectives, experiences and understandings?

In those debates, I could have chosen to be rigid—to say my way or the highway. Instead, both his father and I worked hard to stay open, to stay engaged in the dialogue (and I confess we started some of these "dialogues" deliberately), in order to stay connected with our sons. By remaining flexible, we were able to weave their perspectives and experiences in with our own. Sometimes we changed our attitudes, sometimes our sons did. I did not want to break, nor did I want them to.

Needless to say, now in their twenties, our three sons still keep us aware and flexible about issues that encompass global politics as well as personal ethics. The reward for our flexibility is an ongoing open dialogue with them about right and wrong, about beliefs and values, and to be able to watch as they engage and challenge friends and society, consciously weaving some of our perspectives and beliefs into their own life tapestries.

If we have no attitudes, no beliefs about things, then we are like those off-loom weavings of the 70's, loosely woven with soft fibers and large spaces between both warp and weft threads. When hung on a wall, there was no geometry to the weaving, only amorphous, unidentifiable shape and design. Anything too loosely woven neither warms (too much air space!) nor hangs well—everything slips and slides, defying the viewer to find the focal point or design. This loose weaving does not serve either beauty or function in our lives either.

70

How do we stay flexible in our lives without becoming formless? By creating a strong healthy structure of beliefs and values and then by being willing to reexamine that structure from time to time. If the structure is constricting our ability to grow and change then our attitudes and rules about life may become rigid. Asking ourselves the question, "Does this serve Love? Does this serve Life?" may keep rigor mortis from setting in.

If my primary concern in any situation is what I need to do to have the best possible outcome for others and myself, then I can move from a place of right and wrong to a place of compassion, regardless of how difficult or unclear my choices may be.

The shawls I weave of velvety soft rayon chenille, are softly, snuggly warm. Yet, when placed over a bar and hung from the wall, they become bright banners whose colors warm the wall and the space.

In the same way, compassionate attitudes that serve Life and Love might both look good, beautiful even, to others while also being warmly humane. Instead of hiding and protecting ourselves behind the woven carbon of rigid attitudes, why not choose and offer others the choice of compassion—a brightly colored shawl, a balanced fabric where warp and weft both flex and bend around each other in softness and warmth?

Who wouldn't want to wrap up in that?

THRUMS

- ❧ What old beliefs or attitudes from your past might have become brittle and inflexible?

- ❧ What are more flexible beliefs you can begin to weave into your life to replace them?

- ❧ How willing are you to discuss and evaluate your attitudes? Do you find yourself thinking, if not saying, "My way, or the highway!"?

- ❧ Do you or someone else have this kind of attitude at work? How does it affect everyone's ability to work together? Does time get wasted on power plays instead of on building consensus?

- ❧ Is how you look to the world more important than how you become part of it?

- ❧ What is one of your most strongly held beliefs? What would your life look like if you believed its opposite?

Lesson Nine

Forgiveness— Mending Broken Threads

"As long as you don't forgive, who and whatever it is will
occupy rent-free space in your mind."
~ ISABELLE HOLLAND

"If you haven't forgiven yourself something, how can you forgive others?"
~ DOLORES HUERTA (BARBARA L. BAER)

NE OF THE MOST FRUSTRATING THINGS AS A
weaver is to be weaving happily along, the shuttle
flying back and forth between the warp, laying in
inch after inch of weft, only to discover that I broke a warp
thread several inches back in the fabric. Sometimes this occurs
because of a weak point in the thread. Other times it happens
because something is rubbing on the thread at a point that
causes fraying and then breakage. And sometimes, the tension
on that particular thread is too much and the thread snaps. For
whatever reason, when it happens, the language of a weaver
could compete with that in a men's locker room.

As the weaver, I now do one of three things. If I am lucky
and catch the thread just as it is fraying and before it breaks,
then I slow the pace of my weaving, gentling the beat of the
reed, taking care with the movement of the shuttle back and
forth, until the frayed part is woven safely into the fabric. Then
I continue on with my weaving as if nothing happened.

If the thread is broken, I can decide to just let it drop and continue weaving without it, in which case there will be a gap in the warp that will be either visible or nearly invisible, depending upon the fineness of the threads and the pattern being woven. This is the easiest and quickest solution but is usually not the best for the appearance and integrity of the fabric.

My third choice is to take a large-eyed needle, thread it with a length of the warp thread long enough to reach from a few inches before the break to a few inches past the end of the piece being woven. With the needle, I then must weave that thread into the already woven fabric for a couple of inches, thread that warp through the reed and heddle in the place of the broken warp, and then wind it onto a weighted object so that there will be an amount of tension on that thread equal to that of the others, and let it hang from the back of the loom. This process requires time and a fair amount of patience, but if I value the quality of the weaving then the mending is necessary.

Relationships are both the warp and weft of our life weaving. Early relationships as I mentioned before, make up part of the warp, or foundational threads of our lives. Our family, childhood friends, teachers, and others often move through our lives from beginning to end. As we grow older, we choose the relationships that we will weave into our lives—they are the weft; but whether warp or weft, because we are human, relationships can fray and break. Then we must choose whether to mend that relationship or to let it drop out of the weaving of our life.

One of the hardest lessons for me to learn as a young girl growing into a woman was that, in spite of all my good intentions and my desire to be good and to be liked, I could hurt someone or do something to make someone mad at me.

When I was in college, I was fortunate enough to live on the third floor of a dorm with 12 other young women who grew very close. We shared stories of families, boyfriends, and

74

the struggles with classes. We helped each other home from too much partying, were fiercely defensive of each other, and cried together over failures big and small. That third floor of the dorm was my home away from home, those girls my extended family—until I met the boy who became my husband.

When we started dating, I spent most of my time eating, socializing, and studying with Bob, either in the library or in his fraternity. The dorm became the place where I slept, showered, changed clothes, and went back out again. I saw less and less of my friends whom I assumed were happy for me. But one day, my friend and floormate, Debbi, pulled me into the dorm stairwell for a confrontation. To my shock, she was furious with me! As I listened, I discovered that in my absorption with my newfound love, my friends were feeling neglected, and this one especially was hurt by my lack of care and time spent with her. Unaware, I allowed the thread of our friendship to fray almost to the breaking point.

Human egos and human relationships are fragile threads that, with very little tugging, break. We all want to love and be loved but in our humanity lies our own undoing. No matter how hard we try, no matter how spiritual a life we lead, how much meditation or prayer we do, we will inevitably anger or hurt someone. The challenge is not whether the threads of relationships in our life weavings will break—that is as much a given as are broken threads in a linen warp—but whether or not we are willing to do something to mend those threads.

Saying "I am sorry," and meaning it requires an acknowledgment of our own humanity and our failure to be perfect. We have to admit failing to live up to not just others' expectations of us, but our own expectations as well. Guilt, when we don't let it overwhelm us, is a useful messenger that something is out of balance and action is required.

As I sat in the stairwell listening to my hurt and angry friend succinctly point out just how I had failed to meet her expectations, I had two options. I could let the thread break and fall away from my life's weaving, asserting I had done nothing

75

wrong, that any problem with the relationship was her problem, or I could continue to weave her into my life with a gentle awareness until we had both moved past that frayed point. I chose to weave gently—telling my tearful friend with tears in my own eyes that I was sorry I hurt her, that I had been thoughtless in my recent actions with her, and that I would take more care. Too, she had to adjust her expectations of our relationship and acknowledge the priority of my love for Bob.

The ability to forgive is especially important in a marriage. Long-term intimacy can't fail but to expose the vulnerabilities and character flaws of each partner. Both partners need to be able to acknowledge those vulnerabilities and weaknesses and work with and through them—together—forgiving both themselves and each other. Practicing on forgiving, and even ignoring, the little wrongs like squeezing the toothpaste from the middle instead of the end of the tube, leaving the toilet seat up, leaving lights on in empty rooms, is like plying many fragile threads together—the end result is much stronger and can better resist the sudden and forceful stresses that may pull at the marriage bonds and really test our ability to forgive.

The scary part about forgiveness, of course, whether in marriage or other relationships, is that we leave ourselves open to being hurt again. Yet, if we can't forgive (not forget), then those feelings of hurt, anger, and resentment are like loose threads that slow down our life weaving, wrapping around nearby threads causing them to weaken or break as well, or showing up as skips and errors in the fabric. Those frayed and broken threads of damaged relationships must be dealt with, so that we continue to weave our life fabrics with strength and beauty.

Sadly, sometimes broken threads, broken relationships cannot be mended or woven back into our lives. In fact, because the weaving changes as we weave in new wefts, choice by choice, day by day, sometimes it is better for the beauty of our weaving, if a thread is broken or cut and no longer is part of the fabric.

I have watched both friends and family members struggle through the pain of divorce. One friend, years ago, separated from her husband after discovering he was having an affair. My friend, in her thirties then and raising three young girls, loved her husband and after many discussions and much therapy, forgave him, weaving their frayed relationship back into her life. I was awed by her ability to love him in spite of his actions, and by her ability to forgive. Forgiveness takes amazing strength and humanity.

Sometimes, though, forgiveness also means forgiving oneself for an error of judgment in relationships. We have all entered into relationships with friends or lovers where we later discovered that the person betrayed our trust. Then we need strength to let go of that thread, and a willingness to recognize that a broken thread is no longer critical to the weaving of our life fabric.

Years later, with her daughters grown and out of the house, that same friend discovered that her husband was once again having an affair. This time, as an accomplished artist with a full-time job, grown children, and a new awareness of her own gifts and strengths, she discovered that life without her husband has its own beauty and promise. The thread broke. She will not weave him back into her life even though cutting him from her life will leave a gap. She filed for divorce.

Forgiveness requires the desire for wholeness again. To move towards that place of healing and wholeness takes the ability to move beyond the pain experienced by the self to move into the pain of the other. It requires walking in someone else's shoes.

One of the exercises I use when I teach journal writing is about forgiveness. I ask participants to think of someone they are angry at, hurt by, or just have trouble dealing with for one reason or another. I then tell the participants to write a letter to these people, detailing each wrong word or action. After a break, I ask them to write, with their non-dominant hand, a letter of response from those people they wrote letters to earlier, as if those people were writing the letters themselves. The exercise is usually enlightening for everyone.

Many years ago, one woman in a workshop I was giving at the church I attended as a child, wrote a letter to her sister-in-law because whenever they visited together, it seemed the sister-in-law was bossy and critical of the woman. But after the woman wrote the second letter with her non-dominant hand as if from her sister-in-law, she saw possible reasons for the critical behavior and determined to be less judgmental herself the next time they were together. I received a call from the woman in my class after her next family gathering. She was surprised to find that, without doing anything differently, her sister-in-law was warmer, less critical, and easier to be with.

That is the amazing thing about forgiveness. Sometimes it does not even have to be spoken aloud in order to change the nature of the relationship. Sometimes we can't tell that person because they are far away in distance or time, or because they are not aware of how they may have hurt us, or even because they have died. But the act of forgiveness is an act of restoring wholeness both to the relationship and to the individuals within that relationship.

Letters can be written to those who have died. Dialogues can be held using the empty chair technique of Gestalt therapy, imagining the person who has hurt us sitting in the empty chair across from us while we tell them of our hurt and anger before arriving at a place of forgiveness.

Once again, we can pick up the threads of our present and future to continue weaving without being slowed down or hung up on those frayed or broken threads of the past. Forgiveness restores wholeness to the fabric of our lives and allows us to weave with energy, beauty, and compassion.

THRUMS

- ❧ Think of a person in your life who has hurt or disappointed you. Write a letter to that person relating how hurt you are and why. Then get up, move around, go for a walk. Afterwards, switch hands and write a letter to yourself from that person explaining the situation. How do you feel? Do you understand something about the situation you didn't before?

- ❧ Recall a time you hurt someone. Have you apologized and asked for forgiveness? If not, for whatever reason, what do you need to do to restore balance and wholeness to the relationship and your life? Even if that person is no longer in your life, try writing a letter of apology. Put down all the things you wanted to say but were afraid to at the time. Then create a ritual of release, either through burning, tearing it up, or burying it. How do you feel?

- ❧ Where in your life did you hurt or betray yourself? Have you forgiven yourself? Try the same exercise as above, only using your other hand to write from the perspective of your past self.

- ❧ Sometimes hurt and disappointment in self and others occurs because of unrealistic expectations. Do you hold any expectations in your relationships and for yourself that may be too high for now? For instance, do you expect your grown children to call you several times a week, in spite of their busy schedules and yours? Do you expect all your friends to remember your birthday with a card or a call as a measure of how much they like you? How can you adjust your expectations without betraying your beliefs and values?

Lesson Ten

MAKING MISTAKES—UNWEAVING OR MOVING ON CREATIVELY

"Just because you made a mistake doesn't mean you are a mistake."
~ GEORGETTE MOSBACHER

"Mistakes are a fact of life / It is the response to error that counts."
~ NIKKI GIOVANNI

ORGIVENESS IS A PRACTICE THAT REQUIRES patience, commitment, courage, and humility. Oddly enough, the hardest person to forgive is ourselves. And yet, acknowledging our humanity and imperfections, and then forgiving ourselves for them, is the best way to learn how to forgive others. It is in accepting our mistakes and failures that we more easily understand, overlook, and forgive the mistakes and failures of others.

Is it early in our childhood, when we raise our hand to answer the teacher's questions, only to hear her correct our wrong answer that we discover the discomfort of making mistakes? Or did it start at the dinner table where we said or did something to be part of the circle of conversation and were told to be quiet or to behave? Maybe it even happened in the church where to err is worse than wrong, it's sinful! How does childhood enthusiasm to explore, invent, and investigate, turn into the frozen momentum of fear of failure?

81

Wherever it starts, in the classroom, in the home, in the church, the lesson taught is that making mistakes is undesirable and shameful. Intentionally or not, perfection is reinforced as the goal to be achieved. Many of us strive mightily to reach it or to pretend we have achieved it.

For women, this means a heightened concern about performance in the work place where gender still works against her. One wrong word, one too many absences to tend to sick children, one moment of vulnerability are slips on the ladder that may spell doom for a promising career.

That quest for perfection in the office also reveals itself in an absorption with appearances, shopping for just the right "power" suit, seeking out the best hairstylist for that professional cut and manicure. We work too hard to walk through those office halls looking polished and perfect from head to toe. Our concerns for perfection easily pull us into the advertising vortex of more is better, and spending more is even better, only to discover that we still worry whether or not we are perfect enough. We wear ourselves out competing with the fashion magazines' dictums, meanwhile forgetting that what got us climbing the ladder and hammering on the glass ceiling in the first place were our talents and expertise, not our fashion sense.

As if perfection in the office were not enough to worry about, we have Martha Stewart to thank for feeling inadequate as hostess and homemaker. While she raised creating a lovely home and cooking a good meal to an art, she raised it to a height of perfection never before seen, and undermined our sense of confidence and self-esteem about those roles. Many of us will confess that some part of us wants to be like Martha even as we resent her for setting the bar so high. Worse, we resent ourselves for not reaching it. Yes, we tell ourselves, Martha has a staff to help her do all those wonderful things, and yes, she has money to pay for those wonderful things. Still, we whisper in our mind, "There's something wrong with me. I can't cook/clean/entertain like that!" And that is not a "good thing"!

And motherhood? Forget about it! At least here, Martha doesn't have much to say but plenty of others do, including our own mothers, our aunts, our best friends (whether they have children or not), other mothers, and our own children.

On my refrigerator is a ZITS cartoon given to me by one of my sons. In it, Jeremy's mother is wearing a military uniform with helmet and holding a metal detector on what appears to be a battlefield. Razor wire loops on the ground behind her. Holding the detector, she steps forward and asks Jeremy how things are going at school.

No answer.

Another step and she hesitantly mentions the school calendar and that she has noticed that the freshman dance is coming up. Suddenly the mine detector beeps.

In the next frame the mother uses a knife and pokes at a bump in the ground as she asks Jeremy if he has thought about asking anyo … BOOM!

The final frame is the mother in her usual clothes, with stains on her face and her hair frazzled, coming out of her son's room. The son stands in the doorway with a scowl. The father asks the mother how her fact-finding mission went. She responds, "It's a minefield in there!"

Being a mother often feels like walking through a minefield. After all, making a mistake, any mistake, could mar our kids for life! Can't we just hear them sitting around and telling others the terrible things we did that kept them from …?

I remember, after a heated disagreement, apologizing to our oldest son, Stephen, a teenager at the time, for my overreaction to his behavior. I acknowledged that, despite my best efforts, and because he was my first child that I would sometimes make mistakes (shocking, I know, but there you are …). Stephen turned to me in pique and frustration shouting that that wasn't fair. No, I agreed, it wasn't but then that was life. Parents weren't perfect either.

How much better would we be as partners, parents, friends, employees, and employers if we could humbly admit that, yes,

83

we aren't perfect. We try our best but … Instead, we work too hard, spend too much, and even lie to maintain the façade of our perfection. A perfect example of this, of course, is our political leaders who often fail and fall simply because they cannot admit mistakes. It's hubris—the classical sin against the gods.

Many of the Greek myths contain stories about mortals who dare to claim not only the power, but also the perfection of the gods. Remember that story I mentioned in the introduction about the weaving contest between Athena and Arachne. Arachne made Athena mad not just because she claimed to be a better weaver, i.e. perfect, but because the story she illustrated with her weaving showed Zeus, Athena's father, in his less than perfect love affairs. Athena tore the perfect weaving to shreds and Arachne hung herself. Athena, in an act of mercy, changed the rope into a web and Arachne into a spider. So, Arachne would continue to weave but no longer be a threat to Athena's eminence.

In other cultures, perfection is reserved to the gods as well. The Navaho, for instance, when weaving a rug, deliberately weave a thread into the rug that looks like a mistake. That "mistake" keeps the rug from being perfect and serves as a path for Spirit to enter.

As women, if we accept our mistakes and failures as a path for Spirit to enter then we might take more risks in our work and in our lives. We could stop worrying about perfection and focus on experiencing life. As a weaver, the ideal of perfection will sabotage my choice of colors, my pattern ideas, and slow down my production if I let it. Mistakes are an inevitable part of being an artist, a mother, a woman. How we respond to mistakes makes the difference between an integrated or tattered fabric.

While I was studying for my MFA with nationally known fiber artist, Ferne Jacobs, I wove my symbolic doubleweave pieces and then mailed them to her for critique since we lived on opposite coasts. In the summer of 1983, we finally had a chance to work together. She was teaching a three-week course at Haystack Mountain School of Crafts in Deer Isle, Maine.

Under her auspices, I applied and was accepted as her studio assistant. While I helped her with the class and student concerns, I also warped up a loom and worked on another doubleweave piece.

I quickly discovered that having her nearby while I wove changed the dynamic of my creative process. I wove with more uncertainty than when weaving alone in my studio. I frequently stopped weaving to have her check and critique my work. I became more concerned about doing it wrong, about making mistakes.

By the end of the three weeks, when it was time to pack up and head home, my weaving reflected my worried state of mind. I had woven the first of my tower pieces, Transformation I, but something about the piece felt off. I couldn't put my finger on just what wasn't working in the piece but Ferne spotted it right away. My sense of proportion was off. The figure bursting from the top of the tower seemed too small and contained.

What to do? This was the largest doubleweave piece I had woven, yet, it was not the best, even with Ferne's constant availability. Her suggestion? Cut the warp from the loom, take it home, put it back on my loom, unweave the top six inches and reweave it!!

This was no small task! There were about 200 ends of warp to release, tie, and then, once home at my own loom, rethread and retie onto the loom. Then, I had to unweave those six inches before I could correct them. I faced a long, time-consuming process.

As I stood there in the Haystack weaving studio looking at my piece, I had two choices. I could finish it off as it was, knowing the weaving was less than it could be after already investing hours of work. Or I could do as Ferne suggested, acknowledge the mistake, invest more hours of work and end up with something that truly expressed my abilities and my vision, and pleased me.

Amazed at my insanity, I chose to unweave. Then I finished the weaving, and when I finally cut it from my loom, I knew that the time and effort were worth it. Now, the weaving

85

displayed the power, energy, and excitement I had intended. And, in fact, that weaving is my signature piece. Through the years, as it hangs on my dining room wall, it continues to reveal new understandings of my life. Acknowledging mistakes and being willing to do the work necessary to unweave them brings unexpected rewards. It also requires courage.

When our youngest son, Jason, went through the search and application process for college, he looked at several schools (at the urging of his father and I), but he applied to only one, University of Miami. In spite of encouragement from parents and guidance staff to apply to several, Jason remained firm. He only wanted to go to Miami where the strong music program, the promise of surf and sun, and the presence of a good friend made the choice ideal. Although he wasn't able to enroll in the music program the first semester, Jason was accepted and we packed him up and drove him down to hot and sunny Miami.

Months later, Jason returned home for Thanksgiving with the family. As I stood in the kitchen with Bob, preparing food for the feast, we talked with Jason as he stood petting the dog.

"So, how are you enjoying the sun and school?" Bob asked.

Jason shrugged.

I looked at Bob. "What does that mean?"

"It's OK."

"Just OK? I thought you loved it there?"

"Actually, I think I want to change schools."

I looked at Bob. He looked at me. Eyebrows were raised. Careful, I thought. This is important. Don't blow it with I-told-you-sos.

Gently and with some difficulty, since we were both biting our tongues, Bob and I questioned Jason to discover how unhappy he was at the school and why. As parents who were footing the bill, we could force him to live with his mistake. Or we could let him correct it, either with a lot of complaining from us or with quiet support.

Though Jason made a mistake, we tried not to compound it with our own. We respected the fact that Jason had the courage to admit his mistake in his choice of schools and to vocalize it to us, so we supported his decision. Even though we all knew this meant more work—packing all his stuff up and driving it home, spending hours looking at and applying to colleges again, and even more hours visiting at least one school for music auditions—at the end of the semester, he withdrew from Miami and started a waiting job at a local restaurant while he went through the college search and admissions process all over again.

Though he lost a year of schooling, what he wove for himself in the next four years of college was meaningful and successful. His first choice of colleges was a mistake that could be unwoven. Fortunately, he had the wisdom and maturity to unweave and then reweave.

After I dress my loom with a new warp, before I weave the first weft, I have to weave in a waste yarn in order to evenly space the warp threads at the beginning of the fabric. Sometimes this is a fine thread to create a selvage. Sometimes if I am filling space in warp that will later be fringe, I use bias tape or even toilet paper. This filler is removed later during the finishing process.

The weaving of early adulthood, if we are lucky and have the support and guidance of family and friends, is like that filler. Given the heady experience of making our own choices about what to do after high school, who to date, what job to take, and whether or not to drink ourselves into a stupor at a party, it is not unusual to make mistakes. Some of those mistakes will be like filler at the beginning of the warp—taking up space to help the warp even out so that the weft of the weaving will go smoothly from thereon. Easily removable, yet not really part of the fabric. Some mistakes, like Jason's can be unwoven and rewoven.

Admitting mistakes is a challenge for all of us, requiring that we break old behaviors and ingrained responses. Unfortunately, though we may gather the courage to admit a mistake, sometimes mistakes cannot be unwoven but instead, must become part of the fabric of our lives. The ability to for-

87

give ourselves is strongly tested. Life can change in a moment, and though we often wish for the opportunity to go back, to unweave, often we have only the choice to move forward, to keep weaving. We must fight our way through all the "if onlys," to a place where we stand in the present moment and answer "What next?"

If we develop new skills, create new attitudes, and pick up new threads of courage and understanding, then we can integrate those mistakes into the weaving. Aspects of the pattern of the weaving may change but, with courage, we are able to integrate those mistakes into the weaving as though they were planned.

We all have opportunities to make wrong choices, to make mistakes. For women, issues of whether or not to have unprotected sex which could lead to unwanted pregnancies and disease; whether or not to have an abortion and be haunted by the unlived future; and whether or not to enter into relationship with someone are choices we may discover later are mistakes that can't be unwoven. They alter our lives through physical changes and disabilities, or through emotional or mental scarring.

Many women experience a relationship that is not healthy for them physically, mentally, or emotionally. The mistake is not the relationship itself, which serves as an important teaching, rather the mistake arises when a woman stays in that relationship, a mistake that can have long-term consequences for not just the woman, but for her children if she has them, and for those who love her. Getting out of a relationship where strong feelings of love once lived is difficult and complicated by economic, parental, and legal concerns.

The biggest difficulty and complication, though, is our own willingness to take the blame for everything wrong in the relationship rather than valuing ourselves enough to feel entitled to change our lives for the better. If a partner betrays us, walks out on us, abuses us, then we mire ourselves in questions of what we did wrong. We try to figure out what we can do to make things better. Once out, we then berate ourselves for choosing to get involved in the first place. Instead, we need to congratulate ourselves for our courage in getting out of that relationship, for admitting the mistake and taking action to change it.

The threads of that relationship are part of the weaving of our life. Like the dark foundational threads of the warp, the threads of mistakes remain part of the fabric of our life. In that way, they remain as lesson and warning for future choices. Can we choose more wisely in the future? Will we pick up threads of love, respect, care, and wisdom to weave into our life, creating beauty once again?

Mistakes are part of being a weaver and being human. Mistakes are an opportunity for learning and growing and compassion. We need to give ourselves permission to be less than perfect—to make mistakes, and we need to give others, our friends, our husbands, our children, especially our children, permission to make mistakes as well.

Mistakes are a place for Spirit to enter.

THRUMS

- ⚭ If perfection and not making mistakes is a big concern for you, try this. Look at your calendar and declare a Freedom from Perfection Day. Then allow yourself that day to do things imperfectly. Leave a drawer open, the bed unmade. Squeeze the toothpaste tube from the middle, don't wear makeup. Every time you are about to do something the "right" way, see what it feels like to do it differently. Observe how this makes you feel. Does it open up space in your day for other opportunities?

- ⚭ Can you remember a mistake you made in the past that you were able to unweave? Who supported you in that? Is there someone in your life that needs to unweave a mistake? How can you help them?

- ✤ What choices in the past were filler in your weaving, i.e. mistakes that did not alter your life? If you are a parent, do you allow your children to make "filler" mistakes?

- ✤ Do you have a mistake in your life that you could not unweave? Have you forgiven yourself for it? Have you acknowledged the courage and strength it took to keep weaving your life? What life lessons did you learn from the mistake that help you weave your life with more beauty and wisdom now?

- ✤ Do you have a relationship with a friend or partner that is undermining your physical, mental, or emotional health? What do you need to do to change that? Who do you need to ask for help?

- ✤ When you start to feel anxious about being perfect on the job, as a parent, in a relationship, ask yourself, "Can I give myself permission to be imperfect. Can I leave a path for Spirit to enter?"

Lesson Eleven

COLOR AND TEXTURE—WEAVING IN THE UNIQUE AND VULNERABLE

"Unity, not uniformity, must be our aim. We attain unity only through variety. Differences must be integrated, not annihilated, nor absorbed."
~ M.P. FOLLETT

"Diversity is the most basic principle of creation.
No two snowflakes, blades of grass or people are alike."
~ LYNN MARIA LAITALA

*O*FTEN, WHEN I AM CREATING A THROW COMMIS-
sioned for a client by an interior designer, I must
match fabric swatches whose colors I do not ordinar-
ily work with or like. But, if I refused to work with colors I
didn't like, I would soon not be weaving for that designer—or
any other, for that matter. Instead, I use the commission as an
opportunity to challenge and expand my color palette.

To do that, I must first set aside my prejudices and assumptions about what are "good" colors and color combinations. To
see the potential beauty in these colors, I play with them, opening myself to new perceptions and possibilities.

After looking to art and nature for ideas, I place the colors
I do not like on the floor around me and then add colors I do
like to see how they work together. Often, it is the colors I don't
like that add vitalizing zing to the fabric.

I am not a fan of orange, for instance, but when orange became a popular color in home décor one season, I decided to challenge myself to design and weave an orange throw.

I looked at my thread samples and at the cones of yarns lining one studio wall. I chose three different values of orange, thinking about paprika, persimmons and Persian rugs. With this new frame of reference, I wound on a warp for two throws, using a solid weft for one throw and a variegated weft for the second one. And I was pleasantly surprised with how they turned out. Though they would not be my first choice for my own home, still they were beautiful.

When I do commission work I try to create something that satisfies both the client and me. Sometimes I create just what the designer expected and needed. And sometimes, I create something that really surprises and pleases me as much as it pleases the designer and her customer. When that happens, those color combinations become part of my palette, and I know that my sense of color has grown. In fact, this new perception of color often leads to other designs and color combinations.

I mentioned in a previous chapter the importance of perspective in seeing the big picture of our lives. Perspective, and the ability to temporarily set aside personal likes and dislikes, is also important if we want to weave a life rich in texture with the colors of the local and global community.

We naturally feel safer and more at ease with people who are familiar to us or at least appear to be like us. This kind of clan mentality helped us through the centuries to protect our family and community when survival was a constant concern and we never knew who our enemy—man, beast or weather— would be. Today, when our survival is threatened as much by our technological advances as by man and beast, we easily slip back into that us-against-them clan mentality when we feel ourselves threatened in any way.

For some of us that means choosing gated communities and walled borders. But, if we choose to keep those different from us out of our environment then we are sacrificing the warmth of color and texture for the boring sameness of bed sheets.

Bed sheets are usually woven from cotton or a mixture of cotton and polyester. The quality of our sheets is determined by the number of cotton threads per inch. 180-count cotton sheet has that many fine cotton threads per inch. Higher quality sheets have 200, all the way up to 500 threads per inch, which means the cotton is very finely spun and plied, and threaded very closely together to give a smooth, satiny, yet durable cotton sheet. The same thread is used for both warp and weft. The same color of thread is usually used for both warp and weft, even if we are talking hot orange, pale pink, or bright white. Even though many sheets may have a pretty pattern to them, the pattern is printed on after the sheet is woven.

The reason for using the same fine threads throughout is that, like the Princess in the fairytale of the Princess and the Pea, we do not want to be tossing and turning because our sheets have bumps or a rough texture to them. We want to drift off to the Land of Nod on cool, crisp, *smooth*, sheets.

Wrapping our lives in the sameness of bed sheets leads to a kind of sleep walking. In fact, Native Americans call sleep "the little death". While we sleep, we leave the land of the Conscious and move into the realm of the Unconscious.

Too often we want to stay in that state of little death, of unconsciousness. We want to weave lives of little deaths—that is, we want to weave lives of nothing but safety, security, and consistency. We want every moment of our lives to be like our bed sheets—cool, crisp, smooth. We want our environments, our schools, workplaces, places of worship, our friends to be just like us—to think like us, to act like us, to have the same values and beliefs, to have the same abilities, the same skin color, and even the same God.

To allow people into our lives who are different from us— who think differently, have different values and beliefs—could mean that we might be forced to change our perspective on the world, just like I have to change my perspective on colors I like and don't like when I work with a designer's choice of fabrics for her client. And having to look at and think differently about ourselves and the world around us is always unsettling, and

93

may call us to new understandings, and to making new choices in our life's weaving.

My first strong awareness of having to rethink my understanding of the world, came one day in seventh grade when I stood in the girls' locker room after gym, changing back into my regular school clothes. A classmate stood just down from me getting dressed and talking to one of her friends about how her old man had come home drunk the night before and beat her.

I remember continuing to dress while trying not to let the shock I felt show on my face. First of all, in our Methodist household, alcohol was never present, not even for entertaining. It was an issue that almost split my parents when they were engaged. My mom was used to having wine or such in the house to offer guests. My Methodist dad had been raised that alcohol and drinking were a bad thing and if you didn't believe in its good for yourself, why would you offer it to your guests?

Secondly, though when I was younger I had been spanked (it was still an accepted part of parenting then), my parents never laid their hands on me in anger. I could not fathom the depths of this girl's experience. Though she was wisecracking through the telling, I sensed an abandonment in her words and her need to know why?

At that moment, I understood that everyone did not have my experience and understanding of parenting and family. That, in fact, as I listened to a few other girls commiserate and share in the first girl's experience, my childhood was to be treasured and valued for something not everyone had.

Suddenly a bump had appeared in my bed sheet. This girl's experience had disturbed my comfortable life, and with that small awakening, I became aware of the deeper differences in the world around me.

My bed sheet mindset was completely shredded after experiences in college and especially after my husband and I were married and set up housekeeping that first year in Pittsburgh. My husband, after much searching and frustration, found a job and a one-bedroom apartment just a week before our wedding.

The apartment was a third-floor walk up of a house in the East Liberty neighborhood, close to public transportation.

Owned by an older Jewish couple, the apartment had no door to separate it from the rest of the house—only doors on the individual rooms. I had never before been exposed so intimately to the daily life and customs of a Jewish family, especially an orthodox family.

The wife's elderly and semi-invalided mother lived with them along with their son who had the long hair, beard, and ever-present yarmulke. Many times, throughout the year that we lived there, I heard the wife and her mother yelling and croaking at each other in Yiddish. Many times, I passed the son as we entered and left the home. He neither looked at me nor acknowledged my greeting. Even the smells of their cooking were different.

The first month of married life I spent alone in that apartment while I searched the want ads for jobs. As I listened to the voices on the floor below me, I felt like a stranger in a strange land.

When Bob and I moved to Washington DC so he could attend graduate school at Georgetown, I accepted a job as a subscriber information telephone assistant at a national health insurance company. My first week on the job was in a classroom learning the rules and regulations of health care coverage. When I walked into the classroom the first day, I looked around and saw that not only were all the students women, but they were all African-American. I am not only white—I am pale white—ivory skin tone as the cosmeticians say. I sat down, smiling at everyone yet feeling intimidated and uncertain. Then, the trainer, another white woman, came in, and I admit to breathing a little sigh of relief, and then feeling ashamed for it. I was humbled. What must it be like to experience this and worse on a daily basis?

And yet, we were all women, all waiting to be trained to the same job, all wanting to do well so we could go home with a paycheck to pay bills in order to have a roof over our head and food on the table. Behind the diversity was a unity of purpose and need.

In order to experience an awakening to the richness of diversity we must first step out of our zones of comfort and familiarity. And then we need to appreciate the differences while also looking for our commonalities.

As parents, we often veer away from the different and unique in order to ensure the safety and well-being of our children. When our children entered school, my husband and I went back and forth on the public versus private education dilemma. On the one hand, private schools often insure a more rigorous learning environment, on the other hand, private schools also often insure an insular attitude and outlook.

In the end, we chose to keep the boys in the public school system. We decided that for our family situation, putting ourselves in debt for their early education did not make sense—nor did putting them into a situation where everyone's social, economic, and educational background was similar.

We believed that it was important for them to experience the differences in the life situations of the other students, that some of their friends had it better than they did, and that some of their friends had it worse, sometimes much worse.

Did that mean we had to contend with them bringing home friends whose language, outlook and life goals were different from ours and on occasion, worrisome? Yes. In fact, our oldest son, Stephen, who had never been happy within the school system (and would have been even more miserable in the academic pressures of the private school), often brought home friends whose biggest goal was to just make it through another day of life, or another year of school. Yet, I watched with interest and admiration, as I saw Stephen provide stability and an awareness of broader horizons to these friends whose home lives were often shaky.

One of the things I love about the community we have raised our three sons in is that it is a community woven of an eclectic mix of farmers and millionaires, of blue-collar workers

and professionals, of young and old, of singles and married couples, of straights and gays, of the strong and the vulnerable.

When we were ready to make an offer on the house soon to
be our home, we drove down into the village to the playground
to give our then young sons an opportunity to get out and run
and play on the equipment. There were two older kids there, a
boy and a girl in their early teens who asked personal questions
of Bob and I as we watched the boys play. We answered their
questions briefly, not willing to give too much information
away to two strangers, even if they were kids. Soon, the girl
began cursing and swearing. At first, I was upset. Then I realized something was not normal about her behavior as the
swearing was unrelated to what was going on. Soon, Bob and I
gathered the boys up to return home, uncertain what else to do.

Later, I discovered that the girl had Tourette's syndrome.
Though both she and her brother had mental health concerns,
our small village adapted to and adopted them, weaving them
into the fabric of community life. In return, the community
received the unusual gift of listening to the father as he walked
up and down the streets on summer evenings playing his bag-
pipes.

Older citizens, especially women, have found a safe harbor
here in the village. Whether challenged by ill health, loneliness,
or a tendency to imbibe too much alcohol, they are always
looked out for, driven to shop for groceries, escorted home after
parties, invited to partake of holiday meals. In return, they contribute to the care and mending of books for the local library,
the planting and landscaping of villagers' gardens, and witty
stories and insights where needed.

Through the life of our community, my sons have learned
what it means to grow old, to have very little money, to have
lots, to suffer from loneliness, to die of AIDS, to be born, live
and die in one place, and to know that just beyond the hills lies
a world of difference and adventure. They have grown up with
an extended family of diversity in age, background, race, reli-
gion, and sexual orientation. They have had friends born and

raised in the hills of New York as well as in South America. Small as our community is, diversity is its hallmark and the weaving of that diversity into the community fabric its unique gift. No bed sheets here—but a weaving of marvelous color and texture.

But what if our fear of diversity, of differences pushes us to ignore, deny, or forcibly try to erase those differences? Then we institute programs and policies that however legal and well meaning they may appear, do mental, emotional, and spiritual violence to those who are different from us. Remember when Native American and immigrant children were sent to public schools and forbidden to speak in their native language? We tried to erase their differences. But to erase the differences of cultures, societies, countries, and individuals means we are back to the clan mentality and the rigid attitudes that can result. We are back to bed sheets.

Threads in the warp must be strong to survive the tension on the loom and to absorb the friction of the reed beating back and forth. Weak threads can be incorporated into the warp only if the weak thread is surrounded by stronger ones to support it. Why keep it as part of the warp? That weak thread may contribute just the needed spark of color, shimmer, or texture.

The same is true of human community—if supported by the stronger of us, then the weak and vulnerable among us can offer unique color and texture to the fabric of the community.

The bumpy, fuzzy, stiff or loopy threads that won't work in the warp are often great weft threads—creating interest, color, even excitement to a weaving. Within the weft, beads can be added for sparkle, threads can be looped and left hanging for fringe, metallic yarns can be woven in for added glitz. There is a place in our community weaving for these types of people as well.

One of the things I loved about the movie *Under the Tuscan Sun*, was the variety of people in that Tuscan community and the way the community made room for them—including the single, blond woman who drank too much, had affairs with young men, and often stood dancing and singing in the village fountain. Her gift to the community was the color and excitement she provided—and the community valued it. When we encounter these people, they can enter our own personal weavings and direct them off in exciting and unanticipated ways.

We, too, are threads that weave the fabric of community where we live, work, worship, and play. We offer our uniqueness and the gifts of that uniqueness. We know the importance of having those gifts accepted—how can we refuse the gifts others have to offer?

When I weave shawls for women, they often want a solid color shawl rather than one with four or more colors in it like I often weave. So, I will weave them a solid color shawl, such as a red one. But in that red shawl are at least three values of red so that the shawl has depth to it. In that shawl, I also weave texture by using another yarn that is about three times thicker than my chenille yarn—this texture provides a design focus to the shawl. And in that shawl, I often weave a rayon slub (a yarn that is smooth except for occasional bumps or slubs of color) that is a different color—in the red, I use a gold slub. This provides the spark or accent for the shawl.

I refuse to weave bed sheets for my clients whether the commission is a throw for a designer's customer or a shawl for my own private customer. My clients come to me for color and luxury and excitement, not bed sheets. Those they can get at their local discount store.

I refuse to weave a bed sheet of life for myself or my community either. I don't want to live a small death. I don't want my community to live a small death.

I want to weave in the different, the unique, the colorful, the weak, and the vulnerable.

I want a rich tapestry for my life—not a bed sheet.

THRUMS

- ❧ What walls have you created in your life to keep yourself safe inside while keeping those different from you out?

- ❧ When was the last time you traveled beyond your community, state, country? Did you go off the pasteurized tourist paths and sites? What new perspective on that place and its people or yourself did you come away with?

- ❧ If you have children, what opportunities for experiencing cultural and ethnic diversity do you offer them?

- ❧ What people in your life provide color and texture for you? Who do you provide color and texture for?

- ❧ When you encounter someone who is physically or mentally challenged, how do you greet or interact with them? What spark of color or shimmer do you have to offer each other?

- ❧ At work, how do you and your colleagues value the gifts each has to offer? Is there space and appreciation for differences such as the idiosyncratic and creative person, the person with a physical or mental challenge, along with traditionalist and the bottom-line thinker?

Lesson Twelve

ENDINGS AS BEGINNINGS—
TRANSFORMING LOSS INTO LIFE

"The end of a thing,
is never the end,
something is always being born like
a year or a baby."
~ LUCILLE CLIFTON

"Losing is the price we pay for living.
It is also the source of much of our growth and gain."
~ JUDITH VIORST

IN GREEK MYTHOLOGY, THE THREE FATES, KNOWN in numerous other cultures as Triple Goddess, are the sisters who control each human's life and lifespan. Clotho, as was mentioned earlier, is the one who begins spinning the thread, thus beginning an individual's life. Lachesis, often labeled as the Weaver or Measurer, determines the span and quality of life. Atropos the Cutter, often labeled the Inflexible, cuts the thread of life. Atropos, this most feared of the Fates was also the smallest of her sisters. Why? Is it because at the end of life for most of us, our bones, our bodies have shrunk, curled in on themselves? Or is it because death, the cutting off of our life, is not the huge, fearsome thing we imagine it to be? Is it only those of us left behind to grieve our losses, who imagine death to be a tall, shrouded form reaching for us with skeletal fingers?

101

What would happen to our understanding and experience of loss and death if instead we imagined death as Atropos the Cutter, the crone? Not in the contemporary definition of crone as an ugly, wicked witch, but in the ancient conception of the crone—she who is wise with age. Can we see her as a small grandmotherly figure, bent with age, hair frosted silver, face lined with the wrinkles of wisdom and experience who, like any good Victorian seamstress or needlewoman, carries at her waist a pair of highly ornamented but very sharp scissors? She does not wield those scissors carelessly but with mindfulness and decided determination. She knows that everything begun, a weaving, a story, a life must also have an ending and that endings are her responsibility. Maybe it is the heaviness of the responsibility, to choose the right moment in time to end a life, which has her bent upon herself.

In weaving, unlike some crafts and fine arts, endings are decided with the beginnings, just as the Fates knew the length of each life at its beginning. Atropos always stands with Clotho and Lachesis while I wind the warp for the loom. I must know before I begin winding how long the warp must be for the item or items I intend to weave since I can only weave as much fabric as the length of my warp allows. If I wind a warp that is three yards long, then I can only weave about two and a half yards (depending on the loom) and then the harnesses will no longer separate the threads enough to create a clear shed (that space between threads through which the shuttle moves). Whereas a painter can continue to layer paint, a quilter can add quilting squares and stitches to her quilt ad infinitum, and a potter can constantly reshape the clay until it enters the kiln, once the warp is wound and put on the loom, I can only weave so much until the end of the warp is reached. Nothing more can be woven unless I first unweave (a chore to be avoided!) and then reweave.

And, when I have woven as much of the warp as I can, I must take up my scissors like Atropos and cut the warp threads across the loom until the fabric falls free, and loose threads, the thrums, hang dangling from the back beam's apron.

However fearsome Atropos the Cutter may be, if I did not assume her role and cut the fabric from the loom, the fabric could not serve its purpose. How can my weaving be a shawl to warm a woman's shoulders some cool summer evening if it is still on the loom? How can that scarf drape softly about a man's chilled neck if it is still on the loom? And how can any well-woven fabric be made into a fine coat or fitted jacket unless the scissors are taken up once again? The cut must be made and the fabric removed from the loom, not only so it serves its purpose, but also that another warp may be wound and the loom dressed in preparation for another shawl, or scarf, or jacket. The ending implies and prepares for a new beginning.

Usually, when I take up the scissors to cut the warp off the loom, I am happy to do so for I am usually working under a deadline, and cutting the warp off means that I am that much closer to finishing the garment or throw a customer is waiting for. If the warp is exceptionally long or not one I liked, cutting off of the old warp is a relief because I can dress the loom with a new warp, already wound, and waiting. Occasionally, though, I am not so eager to cut the warp from the loom—I am worried about whether the weaving is successful in design and color; or I am reluctant to sit and tie all that fringe to finish the ends before I wash the fabric. More work! Sometimes, I just do not want to face beginning the process all over again.

On rare occasion, I weave almost to the end of a warp and discover I have not measured correctly and am forced to cut the warp off before I have finished the garment. Angry and frustrated at the work and time invested in weaving a garment that is now incomplete and will be wasted unless I can come up with another way to use the fabric, I still must cut. There is no choice if I want to weave something new.

Cutting off or endings—loss, separation, and death—are as inevitable in life as they are in weaving. Everything comes to an end, and the little endings—the ending of a great day, of a perfect summer season, or even of another year—help us practice and prepare for bigger endings such as parenting, the ending of a relationship, and the biggest ending of all, death. Like reaching the end of the warp before the garment is finished, these ending are something over which we have no control and worse, are often untimely.

Tragically, Atropos' appearance often seems without reason and without justice as in the case of the death of a child. We never stop to think that by giving birth to our children, we welcome in not only Clotho and Lachesis, but also Atropos, or we would never have children. In giving birth, we also give death. I have borne witness to the tearing grief of mothers who have lost their children.

Back in the 80's while attending a three-week session at Haystack, a summer crafts school, I walked into the women's bathroom late one evening, to find a woman standing over the sink, crying. When I asked her what was wrong, she told me that that day would have been her son's twentieth birthday. He had died several years before in a car accident. For her, the grief—and her memories, were still fresh. At times like these, Atropos bears the fearsome visage of the Kali Ma dressed in her skirt of bones, and we would gladly offer sacrifices to her if we could just figure out what it is she would take in the child's place. Instead, the prematurely cut thread of that child's life remains wrapped around the parent's heart, a constant reminder of the loss.

With three small boys of my own, I could only imagine the ongoing pain of this mother - as we all try to do whenever we hear of another child dead of illness or violence. We hold our breaths, fearing that the uninvited fairy, Atropos, will put in an appearance and cast the spell of death on our children. It is every mother's nightmare—literally.

When I turned fifty, I realized I was the age my mother was in 1982 when she was diagnosed with breast cancer and underwent a mastectomy. Then, she seemed older—now I see her as so very young when Atropos took up her scissors and stood waiting in the shadows.

During the next two years following her diagnosis, our

biweekly phone calls to catch up on each other's lives became more frequent as my mother struggled for health and for life, undergoing two rounds of chemotherapy and its attendant nausea, weakness, and loss of hair. Intrigued by my attempts to express myself through thread and loom as she expressed herself through paint and brush, we had conversations about our work mixed in with discussions of childraising. We tried to focus on the positive.

One of the positives was the near completion of my MFA program. The final requirement was a one-woman show that I was organizing at a local conference center's gallery. Among the framed wall hangings I had woven for the show were two weavings of tower images with fire and smoke moving from the bottom to the top, Transformation I and Transformation II. The smoke and fire in the first weaving triumphantly burst forth from the tower into a large dragon/phoenix that breathed its own fire into the sky, while in the second weaving the fire and smoke rose softly from the tower into clouds floating in a calm, serene, sunset sky.

Shortly after the show in the spring of 1984, I began work on another tower piece, putting the warp on my small portable table loom on which I had done most of the other pieces. Weaving in bright colors of greens and red-oranges, I had woven only the first four inches or so when Mom's last battle with cancer began and Inflexible Atropos, as the Greeks called her, stepped out of the shadows.

My father took my mother to the hospital when pains in her neck became unbearable, and discovered that what had been earlier diagnosed as arthritis of the neck was actually the invasion of more cancer. Atropos quietly, slowly snipped at the threads of my mother's life. Trying to stay her hand, radiation was prescribed. My mother now had trouble eating because swallowing hurt and some foods made her queasy.

Anxious to be with my mother and to help care for her, I drove eight hours across New York state with my youngest son, Jason, in his car seat. Because I was going to be there for a week,

105

I brought my small loom and its new piece with me, thinking I would show it to Mom and work on it when Jason went down for his nap.

When I arrived, I found my mother mostly bed-ridden, weak, unhappy, and beneath it all, frightened. I did what any woman does when Atropos begins her work—I tried to affirm life by cooking and cleaning. I waited on my mother, feeding her soft custards and Jellos, ignoring the sounds of Atropos' quiet snip, snipping of her scissors. But I knew she was there and I couldn't weave except for an occasional row to distract my mother and myself.

I watched my father care tenderly for her. I watched good friends come and visit with her, talking about days gone by, trying to engage her and cheer her. I watched and kept thinking, "she's a fighter—she'll get through this." Still, thread by thread, Atropos cut away. I refused to acknowledge her presence. I was not ready for the cutting—the letting go.

The last day of my visit, before I left, I washed my mother while she lay in my parent's double bed. Neither of us was happy that I was leaving. I applied a little make-up to her face to make her feel good and while I worked I talked about Bob and I and the boys coming back for Thanksgiving. She looked up at me and asked, "Do you think I will still be here?"

I was stunned! I had ignored Atropos. Tried to pretend, to deny that she was there, but my mother sensed her presence, had heard the quiet cutting of her scissors. I was young; I did not understand how inflexible Atropos could be. I forced a smile and said, "Of course, Mom, why wouldn't you be?" But her question, and the look on her face haunted me all the way home.

Some weeks later while my mother's older sister cared for her, Mom became incoherent and was rushed to the hospital. The news was grim. The cancer was everywhere. Bob and I and the boys drove back to Pennsylvania, I bringing with me *Transformation II*, the serene weaving I had wanted Mom to have. I wanted it in her hospital room for her to see, hoping its image would give her some kind of peace.

Family gathered round - my father, siblings, cousins, aunts and uncles—coming to see her and, whether they acknowledged it or not, to say goodbye. We knew she was dying—we just did not know how long the process would take. My two oldest boys were to start school in a couple of days, for the middle one it was to be his first day at school and I knew it was important to him not to miss it. So Bob and I made the painful decision to return home, letting each of the boys kiss their grandmother goodbye, I knowing it was for the last time.

Atropos made her final cuts; my mother entered into a coma and then, a couple of weeks later, died. We buried her on a bright and sunny autumn equinox.

Once back home, I could not weave but instead carried within me an image of what I thought would be the next weaving on the loom—a tower leaning or falling to the right, its roots ripped from the soil on the left. That image beat in my heart and in my mind as I grieved. Is it any wonder then, that within the next month, while wearing a pair of my mother's shoes, I sprained my left ankle?

Several months later, my father's father suffered a stroke in his sleep, Atropos cutting cleanly and quickly this time. He never fully regained consciousness, dying just as he had told us he wished to—in his sleep. He was 84 and the loss of my mother, who had been more than daughter-in-law to him, was too much to bear. I stood in the funeral home, greeting people who came to honor Gramps, not sure whether I was grieving for him or for my mother whose loss was still so fresh. That uprooted tower seemed stronger than ever in my mind's eye. And so, as I tried to regain my emotional footing, a few weeks later, while caroling with my son's class, I sprained my left ankle again, metaphor becoming reality.

Several more months went by. Slowly I came back to the loom. To pick up the bobbins of colorful threads and to continue weaving the tower image I had begun the previous spring. As was my style in weaving these images, each row was a decision in color and design. This tower, unlike the previous two, had a stairway winding its way up and around the outside of the tower. Halfway through the weaving, I realized that the points where the stairway was silhouetted on the sides of the tower looked like breasts, disintegrating breasts! In my grief, I believed that when I reached the top the whole tower and stairway were going to disintegrate, falling off into the air.

I continued to dream of my mother. In these dreams, we had the chance to say the goodbyes we couldn't say in the hospital, to give each other a final hug, to share a final laugh. She asserted in one dream that I was the only one who could see her! The dreams were affirming and healing.

I kept weaving away, row by row. And the tower continued to disintegrate, as did the stairway, but when finally I reached the top of the tower, instead of totally disintegrating, the stairway continued its rickety climb into the sky. And when the stairway finally did end, it was not in empty space. Rather, just beyond the last brick of the last stair, only a breath away, in the turquoise sky—stood a door!

I did not know when I began weaving this third tower piece what would be the ending to my mother's struggle with cancer. I had no idea as I struggled to weave in the midst of my grief how long it would take me to finish it, nor that when I did, it would be a resounding affirmation of life, not the surrender to death that that imagined uprooted tower would have portrayed. The doorway in the sky promised a new beginning—for my mother and for me. I named the piece *Transformation III: My Mother's Journey* and knew that she and I had made our own journeys, found our own doors and our own peace.

When I cut that weaving from the loom, I also cut loose my mother, and the worst of the grieving for her. Her loss was the loss of a dear companion, of a wonderful, playful, imaginative grandparent for my children, and of my own personal trailblazer through womanhood. But just as the cutting of the fabric from the loom means the opportunity to weave new fabric, so too Mom's loss meant space for new gifts in my life, including the gift of a gently sensitive, thoughtful, and caring stepmother. Few of us welcome Atropos and her scissors but fearsome as she is, painful as the cutting can be, she brings the opportunity for new life, new beginnings with her.

How do we face Atropos the Inflexible when she enters our lives? How do we bear the pain of loss, separation, and death? How do we find the courage to move forward in our lives that Lachesis is still measuring out for us?

From my own experience, I believe that our culture badly fails at making a place for those who are grieving. During the year following my mother's death, I longed for the days when people wore black as a sign of mourning. I wanted others to know I was wounded, that my heart bled, and that I could not be expected to carry on with life in a normal fashion. I wanted people to be gentle with me, to excuse my lethargy and lack of motivation, to understand my abstraction and forgetfulness, and to forgive my short-temperedness. But, because society did not make room for my grieving, I did not make enough room for it myself. I tried to be strong for my kids who were too young to understand, and to not overburden my husband who worked hard to help me heal. It was only later, at a marriage weekend, that my husband discovered how much hurt and grief I had bottled inside. I often denied opportunities to grieve when they arose and thereby denied those around me the opportunity to support and share.

What did help me to heal from my encounter with Atropos were three things. The first I mentioned earlier, my dreams. Robert Moss, author of *Conscious Dreams*, says those who have died often come to visit us in dreams—to say goodbye, to reassure us of their welfare, and to bring us messages of love and continued care, and so I believe was the case with my many dreams of Mom after her death. Whether you believe as I do, that appearances of the dead in your dreams are often visitations, or that they are just wishful thinking, these dreams heal the heart. Staying aware of your dreams at times of grief, and keeping a record of those dreams is important and helpful.

109

Secondly, though I could not work on it right away, my weaving helped me move from desperation to affirmation. Finding a creative activity such as painting, knitting, redecorating a room, or even singing and dancing, can help the body, mind, and spirit affirm life even in the face of death and can help plot a path out of grief.

Finally, the other thing I did that helped me heal was to keep a journal. I placed no strictures or demands on myself for the journaling but rather wrote when I needed to, either to release the thoughts and emotions churning inside, or to identify just what was going on inside me. At special times, when I most missed my mother and our Saturday phone calls, I wrote her letters. And on some level, I sensed that she read them.

In the midst of it all, I looked for moments of humor and laughter, for if I can laugh then I know life and healing are not far behind. Children and pets are a great resource for that.

Atropos attempts to prepare us for the bigger losses in life through the practice of acknowledging and dealing with the smaller losses. Women especially get to practice endings—the noticeable ending of girlhood when we begin our menarche, the ending of our fertility during menopause. If we learn to move through these with grace and acceptance, then just like the body builder who increases muscle mass by slowly increasing the amount of weight lifted, we become stronger in dealing with the losses of separation and death.

One of those adages that has stood my family and me in good stead over the years is "When one door closes, another opens." In other words, an ending is not just an ending but also an opportunity for a new beginning. Reminding ourselves of this can often help move us past fear and frustration, and into a sense of hope and expectancy. First we have to be willing to look for that open door—or in my case as a weaver, to wind the new warp and dress the loom.

Once we grieve the loss, however big or small, we must continue weaving our life, being with our family, going to work, serving in the community. Lachesis calls us back to the business of life and reminds us to watch for Clotho and the new beginnings that may be coming our way.

Atropos teaches us to be ready for endings, to not leave relationships or responsibilities hanging, to take care of unfinished business as many call it so that we can wake each morning and do as Native Americans do—greet the day with "Today is a good day to die!" For whether we welcome her or no, Atropos stands ready with her scissors, and one day she will move from the shadows to greet us and say, "It is time."

THRUMS

- ❧ How good am I at finishing things? Do I start things and not finish them because I cannot follow through—or because I fear to follow through, to reach an end?

- ❧ What do I need to do to repair relationships important to me? Do I need to tell someone I love him or her? What in my job or home have I been putting off that needs taken care of? What other dangling threads need my attention?

- ❧ How can I begin to practice cutting off, ending? What promises of new beginnings can I see beyond the endings?

- ❧ What do I need to do to move past the grief of endings—keep a dream journal, write unsent letters, make something?

Lesson Thirteen

AGEING AND FINISHING—WEAVING LIFE WITH BEAUTY AND PRIDE

"Age transfigures, or petrifies."
~ MARIE VON ENER-ESCHENBACH

"Old age is not an illness, it is a timeless ascent.
As power diminishes, we grow toward the light."
~ MAY SARTON

"Years are only garments, and you either wear them with style
all your life, or else you go dowdy to the grave."
~ DOROTHY PARKER

I TURNED 53 THIS PAST YEAR. I SAY THIS WITH pride. Everyone who discovers this *says* they can't believe it and that I look younger. I, of course, am happy to believe that they are telling the truth.

I turned 53 this past year. I say this with a special sense of awareness and gratitude because, as you discovered from the last chapter, my mother died at the age of 53, and even now I find it hard to imagine what it must have been like for her to feel so young inside, to have so many more things yet to do like travel to Europe, watch her grandsons grow, watch her other children have children, and yet have to surrender to death, to the cutting of Atropos' scissors.

As I approached my 53rd birthday, everyone wanted to

113

know if I was worried about it—as if I, too, might feel Lachesis measuring my life span and finding it time to give a nod to Atropos. But I didn't—at least not most of the time. Most of the time, I just kept thinking how awful it must have been to be my mother's age and have so much before her, and know death would not let her journey farther.

So, though sometimes I cringe a little when I say it, I more often say it with pride and thankfulness—I am 53.

And each day, when I pass a mirror, I practice acceptance and patience with what that means physically, emotionally, and mentally. For, of course, as much as I appreciate hearing how I look younger than my years, I also know that the tone of my skin, especially on my face, has changed, that my energy levels now go up and down, and that things I could do with ease and even impunity when I was younger, I must pay a price for now.

And yet, as I look in the mirror, examining my face for wrinkles and lines, and am reminded of all the times my mother stood before the mirror examining her own face, stretching her jaw to tighten the skin of her neck, I am also reminded of how ageing and the wear of years softens our edges just as it softens fabrics like cotton and linen.

When fabrics like cotton or linen come off the loom, they are often quite stiff and some are scratchy. Remember what a new linen blouse or shirt feels like—all crispness? Then, gradually, with repeated wear and washings, that crispness disappears and in its places comes a satiny softness that feels like a second skin. Remember the days before pre-washed and stonewashed jeans? Dark indigo, stiff-legged jeans felt as if they could hold you up with their board-like fabric. They would have to go through many, many cycles of washing and drying before they were comfortable. Then manufacturers produced jeans that were comfortable to wear from the first day. They aged the fabric for us before cutting it and sewing it into jeans. No more having to break in our jeans.

Even though chenille yarns are soft and fuzzy on the cone, after the yarns are stretched on the loom and then woven with more chenille yarns under tension, the fabric that comes off the loom is less supple, less soft than you might imagine. Many weavers steam the chenille fabric in order to soften it. I put the fabric in the washing machine on a delicate cycle and let the friction and warm water of the machine soften the fabric and blend the colors and fibers. Then I put it in the dryer to soften it even more and to encourage the fibers to fluff. In this way, I imitate the ageing process. The finished fabric is luxuriously soft and thick, the colors softly blended.

As a young woman, I watched my mother fight the ageing process. She scheduled regular appointments with Evelyn, her hairdresser, to keep her hair colored and styled. I am never going to color my hair, that is just so…artificial, I remember thinking at the time. I watched, too, as she creamed her face night and morning to keep her skin moisturized. I smiled at her antics as she stood before her bedroom mirror, stretching her jaw forward and down, scrunching her eyes closed then opening them wide, and contorting other muscles in her face in order to keep her skin taut and wrinkles at bay. Occasionally, she walked around the house with a white mustache of hair remover above her lip. I thought she was beautiful—I thought all that fuss was unnecessary.

Now, I apologize frequently to her picture that sits on my vanity as I apply moisturizing creams, and check my hairline to determine when I need to make the next appointment to have my hair colored and cut. I watch age spots and stray hairs appear on my face and cringe. Now I understand. I may be 53 years old but what does 53 years old look like? What should it look like? And who decides?

The average life expectancy for women at birth is 80 years. That means we will spend at least half of our lives working to maintain our health and beauty! And if we buy into the ads bombarding us from TV, radio, magazine and the internet, then we will spend a significant portion of our time and money trying to freeze ourselves at age 30 or thereabouts. As weavers of our lives, our challenge is to continue weaving lives of meaning and passion while also allowing age and wear to soften our edges, to make us more flexible rather than less, and to add the embellishments that make us interesting and exciting to know and be around.

In ancient times, and in many ethnic cultures today, older women are considered the holders of wisdom and power, and honored as the crone. The crone is the third of the trinity of the Triple Goddess—maiden, mother, and crone. She is exemplified in goddesses like Athena, Metis, and Sophia. The belief was that once women stopped menstruating, they held the lunar blood, the "wise blood" within, and thus retained the wisdom to offer to and guide others. Their role is to show others the way, how to live and survive, how to live and love well.

In many societies, "grandmother" is a term of respect for older women, denoting their wisdom and ability to nurture others. In this country, we are just as likely to use the term "granny," and use it as a pejorative that diminishes the gray-haired elder into a little (see, a diminutive!) old lady who has nothing to offer us other than her need for increased physical and mental care.

Who can blame women who continue to color their hair into their 70's and beyond? Once gray, we fear becoming the little old lady rather than the wise and powerful crone. Men struggle with ageism as well, but we all know that many men get better looking as they get older. For instance, I actually prefer the look of the older Sean Connery. And frankly, Pierce Brosnan was cute when he was a young Remington Steele, but he is deadly good-looking now—James Bond or not! Society uses labels like "experienced" and "mature" for men like these of a certain age, while women are just labeled "old."

I am happy to be alive and intend to celebrate many more birthdays, but every time I pass a mirror, I find myself sympathizing more and more with Snow White's stepmother. Having your mirror tell you, whether by reflection or saying it aloud, that you are not the fairest in the land is disconcerting to say the least!

Of course, each of us has our own definition of beautiful as well as our own line we draw in the sand when it comes to where we will not let the ageing process change us. Some of us want to go au naturel all the way, from our hair to the lines and wrinkles on our face. Others will spend whatever it takes for facial peels, make-up, hair coloring, and even plastic surgery in order to continue to feel good about ourselves. And others, like myself, will find ourselves somewhere in the middle of those two ends of the spectrum.

When I first colored my hair, I did so for two reasons. I felt 40 was too young to have gray hair, and because, as someone selling handmade fashion, I knew I had to look my best in my booth. With my pale skin, I did not believe that gray hair would do anything but make me look older and tired.

Of course, now at 53, I still feel too young to have gray hair and I have a sense that looking at a gray-haired self in the mirror each day will make me feel older, not better or wiser. Now that most of the responsibilities of motherhood are finished and I am focusing on my career as writer, weaver, and speaker, I find I care more about my weight, my hair, my makeup, and clothes than I did when I was young. I have more time and a little more money to spend on wardrobe and my appearance, and that is a good thing, since looking good as we age usually takes more time and effort.

Tempting as it is to judge other women for the lack of or excess in their beauty routines, the truth is that beauty is in the eye of the beholder. We are each that beholder. We have to please ourselves first. If one of us feels beautiful after much pampering and primping, and the other feels beautiful after nothing more than washing our face and brushing our hair, that is all that matters. We need to give ourselves and each other permission to do what makes us feel good, what makes us feel beautiful as we grow older. Recognizing what clothes, what colors, what beauty routines, help us feel good about ourselves is part of the power of self-knowledge that comes with age.

After all, the question is not whether we will grow older. If we maintain our health, we will all grow older. The question is *how* will we grow older? Will we grow wiser and more power- ful in that wisdom? Will we soften, become less stiff, more flexible? Will our inner beauty shine through? Or will we, like antique silk, dry out, become brittle and shatter?

As we grow older it is important to not only feel comfort- able with what we do to make ourselves feel beautiful, but we also need to choose good role models, whether celebrity or family member, for ageing.

I am fortunate in that I have great role models both for how and how not to grow older. My maternal grandmother mod- eled for me how not to grow older. As a woman, she worked hard raising three daughters, and then worked full time after her divorce from my granddad. While she was middle-aged and working, she enjoyed being with friends and family. She played bingo and bowled. She liked going out to dinner and a movie with her gentleman friend. But as she grew older, her life seemed to shrink around her. After her retirement, she spent most of her day in front of the TV, watching soaps and game shows and the news which made her increasingly unhappy. Living in a suburb of Washington D.C., she easily fastened and focused upon the crime and violence around her. After the untimely death of my mother, I watched my grand- mother decline in mental and physical health, her horizons shrinking, her mind and body drying up until, like antique silk, she shattered and died. I loved my grandmother and I am thankful for the example she gave me of how not to grow older.

Her daughters, on the other hand, I watch carefully, making mental notes of how to grow older in their ways.

My mother's older sister, Indira, is in her mid-70's and just in the last three years she started an environmentally conscious nursery business and has built or bought, remodeled and sold several homes! As she ages, she constantly looks for good busi- ness investments, plunges into new learning opportunities, and stays curious about metaphysics, politics, and life in general. She is still a force to be reckoned with in her family and her community. For her, the world is still a good place to live.

Her younger sister, my aunt Sandy, recently turned 60. I have a hard time believing that as I occasionally have a hard time believing I am 53. Her eyes are still bright with the vitality and curiosity she had at 30. When I last visited her, she took me with her to her yoga class. I had not practiced yoga for some time, so I panted in admiration while watching Sandy move confidently through most of the postures. After lunch we returned home to her townhouse that she just redecorated, doing much of the work herself. Now that she is retired after working for most of her life to support herself and her two daughters and son, she goes to movies, attends concerts, visits craft shows and celebrates family events with her children and Indira's who live in the area. She is always ready to travel and explore new opportunities.

I watch these two women, the sisters of my mother, as they stay involved and passionate about the life around them and I remain optimistic about my own ageing.

Thankfully, my father and stepmother, Gail, are also good role models. Since retirement, my father has learned to play piano, paint in oils, repair clocks, and speak in Spanish. He and Gail also sing in the church choir and participate in a church study group, reading and discussing books and ideas by leading progressive theologians. Their schedules are full of learning, travel, and friends and family. Life remains for them a rich tapestry.

All of these role models are growing in mind and spirit while their bodies soften with age. The fabrics of their beings shine with the beauty of wear. They are transfiguring with age, not petrifying, not shattering. They are also modeling for me how to cope with the physical limitations that appear with age.

These limitations sneak up on us. First, we can't stay up as late as we used to without paying for it in fatigue the next day. Next, remaining in one position too long causes muscles and joints to complain when we finally do move. Soon, like parts wearing out in a car with high mileage, first one ailment, then another sends us regularly to our doctors for mending and relief.

119

As one grows older, life is a series of adjustments and accommodations. My stepmother suffered through a summer of pain because of back problems. Although she was frustrated with the pain and her inability to be her usually active self, she stayed patient with the process, taking the medication, visiting the doctors and then finally undergoing surgery. The surgery relieved the pain, and gave her back most of her mobility but not all of it. She has made adjustments with humor and grace.

My aunt, Indira, slowed her pace this past year when fatigue and stress from business and family zapped her energy. Reading about different healing modalities, exploring herbs and other treatments, she worked toward health. Some days she was ready once again to change the world. Other days, though she was barely able to get out of bed, she used the time to read and plan her next venture. She is learning to parcel out her energy and to safeguard it in order to do the things she really wants to do. What I am learning as I watch her is the need to change the focus of our lives as we age from doing to being, as well as practicing patience as we move back and forth between those two states.

As we discussed in the chapter on structure, these physical limitations or challenges also offer freedom. Growing older often means a lessening of demands on our time and energy. Many of us retire from full-time employment. Most of us are done with child-raising. Though our energy may be less than what it was, we usually have more control of how we use it. Many of us have more control of our financial resources, while others of us are struggling to find enough money to pay for food and shelter.

Sometimes, when I weave and I am uncertain what I want to weave into the next few inches of fabric, I loosen the ratchet on the cloth beam (the roller that takes up the woven cloth) and unwind what is already woven so that I can achieve a sense of the direction of the weaving and determine what comes next.

For those of us 50 and older, we can look back at our lives, unrolling the fabric of memories and photos, rereading our journals, and listing our accomplishments. From this long-range perspective on our life, we gain clarity about who we are and how the weaving of our lives is progressing. We are more certain about what works in our lives and what doesn't, what we like and what we don't like, what is important to us and what isn't. We feel the passage of time and know that if we have dreams yet unfilled that we need to take action on them today, not in some fuzzy tomorrow.

The leading edge of women of the baby boomer generation are now transitioning out of middle-age into what I call the crone years. In the next ten years, for the first time in history, the group of women over 50 will be the largest it has ever been in this country. According to statistics, these women will also control a significant portion of financial resources as a result of inheritance and ownership or controlling interest in companies.

With clarity and wisdom comes power. With financial resources comes power. With large numbers comes power.

We must ask as we age, how will we use our power? How do we move from doing to being in this place of power? Can we role model for others, especially younger women, how to make healthy and loving life choices, as my aunt Sandy does by taking her yoga classes. Can we model how to continue to contribute to society with our knowledge, our understanding, and our compassion like my stepmother did when she volunteered for a reading program for elementary age children. Can we model how to use our power and perspective to improve our social and political environment as my aunt Indira does by writing letters to the editor and contributing to political causes?

Ageing is a time to redefine beauty, to choose successful role models for ageing, and to use the power of our wisdom and resources to nurture our families, friends, and the world. As we look back on what we have already woven, we know we have the power to weave even more beauty and love into our lives.

121

THRUMS

- ❧ Today, whatever your age, what do you like about your appearance right now? How will that change as you age? What will you do about it?

- ❧ Do you find yourself judging other women for giving too much or not enough attention to their appearance? Why? How would you feel about yourself if you did less or more for your beauty regimen?

- ❧ Do you have any role models among your family or friends for ageing? Who? What do they teach you, good or bad, about growing older?

- ❧ What older female celebrity, political leader, or businesswoman do you admire? What do they teach you about using wisdom and power for community and society?

- ❧ Regardless of your age, try to imagine what your ideal life looks like when you are 60, and 70, and 80. What do you need to do now, such as exercise, invest in an IRA, start a savings account for travel, in order to make growing older both a reward and an adventure?

- ❧ What can you do now and in the future to use your wisdom and your power to make life better for others—write a letter to the editor; teach someone to read, or cook, or sew; educate yourself politically and then exercise your right to vote?

Passing on the Shuttle

MENTORING THE DAUGHTERS OF OUR HEARTS

"Biology is the least of what makes someone a mother."
~ OPRAH WINFREY

"Knowledge ... always imposes responsibility."
~ W.M.I. JAY

*Y*OU ARE PROBABLY WONDERING WHAT I, AS THE mother of three sons, has to say about mentoring daughters. I have to admit, all those years of playing with dolls and imagining being married and having my own babies, I never thought I wouldn't have at least one daughter. I also have to admit, that I would not change the way things turned out. After all, I already knew a lot about being a girl and very little about being a boy. My sons taught me quite a lot.

And yet, on occasion, I think about how close I was to my mother. The special relationship we had that, before my mother's death, was turning from parent and sibling to older friend and younger friend. With her absence from my life and my own lack of daughters, I have had to redefine the mother-daughter relationship.

When my mother died, my aunts and then my stepmother lovingly stepped in, not to fill the void but certainly to lessen it. My mother's older sister, Indira, flew me out to California to

123

attend a retreat on grief and healing with her, strengthening a bond that continues to grow. My father's younger sister, Aunt Fran, generously invited me along with my husband and three young sons to come visit her and my uncle for Easter vacation those first couple of years after Mom died. My mother's younger sister, Sandy, who feels more like my older sister than my aunt, every year invites me to stay with her whenever I am exhibiting at a craft show in the area, and like my mother, takes great pride in my weaving and other ventures. She happily shares stories and memories with me of my mother.

My stepmother, whenever she visits us with my father, pitches in to help weed the jungle that is our yard. One year she arrived with new cookie sheets and potholders for me having noticed my other ones were well-worn, something only a mother normally notices.

None of these women tried to replace my mother. They all knew what an impossibility that was. But what they did do was expand my understanding of the word. Up to that point, I thought I understood clearly what a mother was. After all, I was a mother of three boys. I even had a small understanding of the word in its verb form—to mother. To mother is to give birth to, to protect as a mother, to give rise to, to be the source of.

My aunts and later, my stepmother, protected me from pain and loneliness, gave rise to healing and wholeness and under-standing, and were the source of new connections, new relationships and new love. They were my mentors—experi-enced and trusted advisors. I knew their love, care, and understanding were only a phone call away. I had become a daughter of their hearts.

I am lucky. As I know from my own experience as a substi-tute teacher, too many young women are without healthy role models, without mentors, and without mothers. Too many women of all ages and backgrounds are without mentors and mothers of the heart. With our highly mobile society, few of us live close to extended family. The days of mothers, grandmoth-ers, and aunts guiding, advising, and protecting a young girl's growth into adulthood and the world are waning or gone. One of the stresses of today's woman is the lack of familial support systems, while struggling to balance career and family, especially for single mothers. We have the power to change this.

Over the centuries, women's knowledge, wisdom, and skills have been passed from mother to daughter to granddaughter. In this way a young girl growing into womanhood, learned how to cook, to raise children, to gather and use herbs, to quilt, to spin, and to weave. Personal treasured recipes for jam, for a quilt pattern, a healing salve, and for a woven pattern were handed down from generation to generation. Sometimes, young women other than daughters were taken under a woman's tutelage to learn her special knowledge so if the woman did not have daughters of her own, the knowledge and skills would not be lost, or because "many hands make light work."

As women, if we have mastered anything—how to be in relationship, how to cook, how to raise happy, healthy children, how to succeed in the corporate environment, how to write a poem—then we have the opportunity and the responsibility to share that with other women, older and younger. Daughters of our hearts can be any age! We can share it with our nieces and daughters-in-law, or with friends and acquaintances—but our knowledge, our mastery (or misstery!) needs to be shared.

Even more important to pass on than our knowledge and skills, however, is a sense of self-worth. For those of us who understand that, regardless of our mistakes, our failures, and our shortcomings, we have intrinsic value and something to offer the world, we need to hold up this mirror of self-worth to other women, especially young women, so that they see shining back at them the light of their own beauty, value, and gifts

Once we understand that our value is not determined by our dress size, the quality of our manicure, the title on our office door, but by who and how we love, then it is incumbent upon us to role model this for other women. . If we learned how to weave lives of beauty and wisdom and love, then we must share that with other women who want to do the same.

I count myself blessed each day for a marriage that continues to be an adventure and a delight. Bob and I have worked hard at it to make it so. I have cousins and friends who look at my relationship with Bob and see it as a light of possibility and promise for their relationships. We serve as role models for a loving and committed marriage.

I share this with you because, while I am proud to be approaching 33 years of marriage to my husband, I also know that Bob and I serve as role models. This is a scary and humbling responsibility. And it is a responsibility I accept and cherish.

In fact, to celebrate our 25th wedding anniversary, Bob and I invited friends and family, and members of our original wedding party, to join us for a celebration that included a renewal of vows followed by a dinner with music and dancing. We were celebrating for two reasons. One reason was gratitude—to thank our family and friends for supporting us through those 25 years of marriage. A marriage does not thrive on its own.

The second reason for the gathering and celebration was to show the younger generation of our sons and their friends, and of our nieces and nephews, that a long-term, committed marriage was possible. To emphasize that point that evening, we gave the other couples in attendance who were married for 25 years or more, red carnations to wear, thus identifying them to others. These couples included Bob's best friend and best man, Bill, and his wife, Patty, my matron of honor, Dotti, and her husband, Zeke, along with aunts and uncles, and friends from our village. We hoped the number of couples wearing red carnations were encouraging and affirming as role models.

To mentor and to mother is first of all a call to role model. As partners and wives, we can show other women the importance of expecting only the best for ourselves within a relationship. As literal mothers, we can role model how to parent with love and patience. As women with vocations and avocations, we can role model how to follow the creative passions of our hearts and how to move into the corporate world without losing our hearts and souls.

As mentors and mothers, another responsibility is to listen —without judgment, without an attempt to fix or change— just listen. Mothers get into the habit of kissing and making better. We always want to heal and fix. With daughters of the heart, we are more often called to listen rather than fix. Listening is magic. To listen with your entire being, with heart and mind and soul engaged, is to offer back the healing balm of recognition, of acceptance, and of compassion.

Encouragement is another task of mentors and mothers. It is not enough to blaze the trail, we have to cheer and shout support as others follow our path. We all need words of encouragement. One of the things I missed most after my mother died was her role as my cheerleader. We need to cheer each other on, especially when the challenges are tough and energies are flagging. One word of encouragement can make a difference.

Finally, as all mothers know, the most important thing to do, to offer, is love. Love may manifest as babysitting for an hour so a busy, frazzled mom can have a nap or a luxurious bath. Love might take the shape of a meal for a friend who is working overtime on a project to meet a deadline. Or love may simply be the offering of a shoulder for a good cry and a hug afterwards.

Each of us brings our own unique gifts and expressions to the roles of mentor and mother. However we do it, whatever shape it takes, we need to pass on the shuttle, to show others how to weave a life of beauty.

With this book, I hope I have fulfilled, to some extent, my responsibility to mentor to you, to pass on some of the secrets of weaving a woman's life that I learned while weaving yard after yard of fabric and of life.

So, my blessing as your weaving teacher is: With each throw of the shuttle and each beat of the reed, may the fabric of your life grow more beautiful and strong, and may the bright threads of your dreams, waking and sleeping, glow and glitter, and bring bright blessings on yourself and others.

May it be so.

127

THRUMS

- ❧ Who are some of the women in your life who have mentored you? What have you learned from them? Have you expressed your gratitude to them?

- ❧ Who are some of the women, of any age, in your life whom you can mentor? What are your gifts that you can pass on?

Appendix A

LANGUAGE OF THE LOOM

*W*HILE MANY TERMS FROM THE CRAFT OF weaving have insinuated themselves into our everyday language, there are still some terms that you may be unfamiliar with or unclear about. So here are some definitions and even an illustration to refer to as needed. The weaving terms are simple and less confusing than the terminology of the computer—even though the loom is the ancestor of the computer. Amazing, isn't it? Well, think about how a bit is either on or off—so a harness is either up or down. What's a harness? Read on!

Warp–These are the threads that run vertically in a fabric. These are also the foundational threads of the fabric and therefore need to have some strength for the measure of tension they will be under. When you read *warp* think up and down and generally strong.

Weft—These are the threads that are horizontal in a fabric. They can be almost anything and are wound on a shuttle in order to move back and forth between the warp. When you read *weft* think back and forth and individualistic.

Shuttle—No, we are not talking space shuttle or airport shuttle, though the principle is the same—it serves to carry something back and forth, in this case the *weft* threads. So, when you read *shuttle* you could think of space or airport, but—not to confuse you—most shuttles are either called *boat shuttles* (because they look like a boat) or *ski shuttles*.

Looms—There are all kinds of looms—some very simple and portable, some very large, as large as a whole room, and very complicated. The basic job of a loom is twofold. One is to keep the warp threads straight and taut, and the other is to open a path or shed between the warp for the weft to pass through.

Now here is where things get a little tricky—the parts of the loom will be referred to in the lessons, so here is an illustration of a loom that might help you better understand the terms.

(See illustrations on facing page.)

Harnesses and heddles—Like a harness controls a horse pulling a load, the *harnesses* of the loom control the threads and their movement. As the threads of the weaving come up the back of the loom to the front, the threads travel through a kind of vertical needle with a hole in the middle called a *heddle*. These *heddles* are kept in order by each *harness*. A handloom may have anywhere from two *harnesses* up to twelve.

Treadle—These are found on floor looms only and control, with foot pressure, the raising and lowering of the *harnesses*.

130

Shed—No, this is not the shed in your backyard giving shelter to the lawnmower. In this case a *shed* is the space between *warp* threads created by the raising and lowering of *harnesses*.

Reed—The easiest way to remember and think of this is as a comb. What the *reed* does is keep the threads evenly spaced and help beat the *weft* into the web of woven fabric.

If this all sounds a little technical, don't worry. There will not be a test later. If you really want to understand weaving just remember all those loop potholders you made as a young girl. That metal frame with all those wicked teeth was the loom. The loops that went on first were the warp. And those other loops that had to be woven so carefully over and under the first loops were the weft.

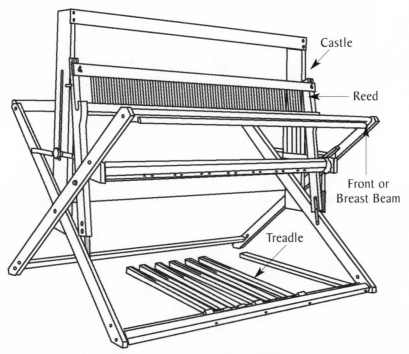

Castle

Reed

Front or
Breast Beam

Treadle

FRONT VIEW OF FOUR-HARNESS FLOOR LOOM

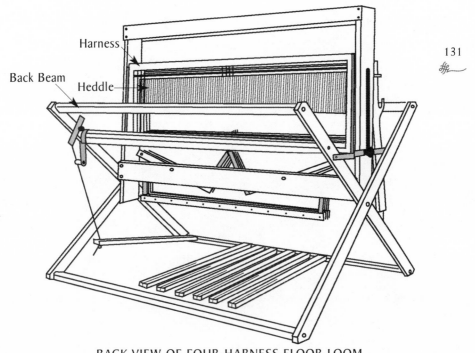

Harness

Back Beam

Heddle

131

BACK VIEW OF FOUR-HARNESS FLOOR LOOM

And remember those paper weavings you did in elementary school from construction paper? The cut rectangle of paper was both your loom and your warp (and wasn't it frustrating when one of the strips of your "warp" tore?) The strips of paper that you then wove in and out were your weft.

This is how basic weaving is—vertical and horizontal threads that create fabric in an over-under pattern. This structure and pattern appears in many configurations throughout our lives—which is why it is such a good metaphor for our lives as women.

$$\mathscr{A}ppendix \ \mathscr{B}$$

RESOURCES

*L*ISTED BELOW ARE BOOKS, ORGANIZATIONS, AND other resources, some of them mentioned in the previous pages, that I am personally familiar with and find valuable. I hope you will too.

BOOKS

Creativity:

Arrien, Angeles. *The Nine Muses: A Mythological Path to Creativity*. New York: Jeremy P. Tarcher/Putnam, 2000.

Cameron, Julia. *The Artist's Way: A Spiritual Path to Higher Creativity*. New York: Jeremy P. Tarcher, 1992.

———. *The Vein of Gold: A Journey to Your Creative Heart*. New York: Jeremy P. Tarcher, 1996.

———. *Walking in This World: The Practical Art of Creativity*. New York: Jeremy P. Tarcher, 2002.

Mountain Dreamer, Oriah. *What We Ache For: Creativity and the Unfolding of Your Soul*. San Francisco: HarperSan-Francisco, 2005.

Dreams:

Burch, Wanda Easter. *She Who Dreams: A Journey Into Healing Through Dreamwork*. Novato, CA: New World Library, 2003.

Delayney, Gayle. *All About Dreams*. San Francisco: Harper-SanFrancisco, 1998.

Mellick, Jill. *The Art of Dreaming: Tools for Creative Dream Work*. Berkeley, CA: Conari Press, 1996.

Moss, Robert. *Conscious Dreaming*. New York: Crown Trade Paperbacks, 1996.

Journal Writing:

Baldwin, Christina. *Life's Companion: Journal Writing as a Spiritual Quest*. New York:Bantam Books, 1991.

Hinchman, Hannah. *A Life In Hand: Creating the Illuminated Journal*. Layton, Utah: Peregrine Smith Books, 1991.

Schiwy, Marlene A. *A Voice of Her Own: Women and the Journal-writing Journey*. New York: Fireside, 1996.

Mythology, Fairytales, and History:

Arrien, Angeles. *The Tarot Handbook*. Sonoma: Arcus Publishing Company, 1987.

Barber, Elizabeth Wayland. *Women's Work: The First 20,000 Years—Women, Cloth, and Society in Early Times*. New York: W. W. Norton & Company, 1994.

Bolen, Jean Shinoda, M.D. *Goddesses In Every Woman: A New Psychology of Women*. NewYork: Harper Colophon, 1984.

von Franz, Marie-Louise. *Problems of the Feminine in Fairytales*. Dallas TX: Spring Publications, Inc., 1972.

Walker, Barbara G. The Woman's Encyclopedia of Myths and Secrets. San Francisco: HarperSanFrancisco, 1983

Warner, Marina. *From the Beast to the Blonde: On Fairy Tales and Their Tellers*. New York: First Noonday Press, 1996.

Rituals:

Biziou, Barbara. *The Joy of Ritual: Spiritual Recipes to Celebrate Milestones, Ease Transitions, and Make Every Day Sacred*. New York: Golden Books, 1999.

Women's Issues:

Arrien, Angeles. *The Second Half of Life: Opening the Eight Gates of Wisdom*. Boulder, CO: Sounds True, 2005.

Edwards, Paul and Sarah. *The Practical Dreamer's Handbook: Finding the Time, Money, & Energy to Live the Life You Want to Live*. New York: Jeremy P. Tarcher, 2001.

Kubler-Ross, Elizabeth. *On Death and Dying*. New York: Scribner, 1997 (reissue).

Miedaner, Talane. *Coach Yourself to Success: 101 from a Personal Coach for Reaching Your Goals at Work and in Life*. New York: McGraw-Hill, 2000.

Orloff, Judith, M.D. *Dr. Judith Orloff's Guide to Intuitive Healing: 5 Steps to Physical, Emotional, and Sexual Wellness*. New York: Times Books, 2000.

Richardson, Cheryl. *Take Time for Your Life: A Personal Coach's 7-Step Program for Creating the Life You Want.* New York: Broadway Books, 1998.

Roberts, Cokie. *We Are Our Mothers' Daughters.* New York: William Morrow and Company, Inc., 1998.

Rountree, Cathleen. *On Women Turning 40: Coming into Our Fullness.* Santa Cruz, CA: The Crossing Press, 1991.

————. *On Women Turning 50: Celebrating Mid-Life Discoveries.* San Francisco: HarperSanFrancisco, 1994.

————. *On Women Turning 60: Embracing the Age of Fulfillment.* New York: Three Rivers Press, 1998.

————. *On Women Turning 70: Honoring the Values of Wisdom.* San Francisco: Jossey-Bass, 1999.

Williamson, Marianne. *A Woman's Worth.* New York: Ballantine Books, 1993.

Learning and Retreat Centers:
Haystack Mountain School of Crafts, Deer Isle, ME.
  www.haystack.org
Kripalu Center for Yoga and Health, Lenox, MA.
  www.kripalu.org
Mount Madonna, Watsonville, CA. www.mountmadonna.org
Omega Institute for Holistic Studies, Rhinebeck, NY.
  www.eomega.org

135

Organizations:
eWomenNetwork, Dallas, TX. www.ewomennetwork.com
International Women's Writing Guild, New York, New
  York. www.iwwg.org
Mythic Journeys, Atlanta, GA. www.mythicjourneys.org

Weaving Resources:
Handweavers Guild of America, Inc., 678-730-0010,
  www.weavespindye.org
Fiber Studio, 603-428-7830, www.fiberstudio.com
Handwoven Magazine, 970-669-7672, www.interweave.com
Fiberarts Magazine, 800-875-6208,
  www.fiberartsmagazine.com
Schact Spindle Company, Inc., 303-442-3212, www.schactspin-dle.com

About the Author

PAULA CHAFFEE SCARDAMALIA is a professional writer, weaver, dream and creativity coach. She contributes regularly to "Crafts Business Magazine" and writes book reviews for *Foreword Magazine* and *Broadsheet*. She is a member of the International Women's Writing Guild (IWWG) and teaches writing and shamanic dream work at their annual international summer conference.

Paula sells her luxurious and colorful handwoven rayon chenille throws, pillows, and wearables through her business, Nettles and Green Threads (the name is taken from a fairytale).

She weaves the threads of her experience as weaver, writer, creativity and dream coach together to teach, inspire, and guide other women on the inner path of spiritual and creative exploration. She offers lectures and workshops on a variety of spiritual and creative topics.

She lives with her husband, Bob, and Duncan, their collie, and Chino, their cat, in an 1840's Greek Revival farmhouse needing constant attention in the foothills of the Catskills in the historic hamlet of Rensselaerville, NY.

You can visit the author at www.weavingthedream.com.